Also by LeAnne Howe

Shell Shaker

Evidence of Red

Miko Kings

CHOCTALKING ON OTHER REALITIES

BY
LeAnne Howe

Foreword by Dean Rader

aunt lute books | San Francisco

Aunt Lute Books
P.O. Box 410687
San Francisco, CA 94141
www.auntlute.com

Cover design: Amy Woloszyn, Amymade Graphic Design
Cover photo: Jim Wilson
Text design: Amy Woloszyn, Amymade Graphic Design
Interior Illustrations: Ellen French
Author Photo: Jim Wilson

Senior Editor: Joan Pinkvoss
Managing Editor: Shay Brawn
Production: Laura Chin, Learkana Chong, Ellen French, Lisa Hastings,
    Taylor Hodges, Alexa Kelly, Kara Owens, Erin Peterson, Allison Power

This book was made possible with support from the National Endowment for the Arts, the San Francisco Arts Commission, the Vessel Foundation, and the Sara & Two C-Dogs Foundation

Library of Congress Cataloging-in-Publication Data

Howe, LeAnne.
   [Essays. Selections]
   Choctalking on other realities / by LeAnne Howe ; foreword by Dean Rader.
      pages cm
   ISBN 978-1-879960-90-9 (pbk. : acid-free paper)
   1. Howe, LeAnne. 2. Indians of North America. I. Title.
   PS3608.O95A6 2013
   814'.6--dc23
   [B]
                             2013032092

Printed in the U.S.A. on acid-free paper

10 9 8 7 6 5 4 3 2 1

It is a little known fact that Choctaws are thrill seekers.

Contents

Foreword

"Scary isn't it," writes LeAnne Howe in her essay that chronicles her trip to Japan, "how one narrative bleeds into another—from Ronald Reagan to Pearl Harbor to my grandmother's Japanese china."

By "scary," LeAnne means "not scary."

By "scary," she means "cool."

By "scary," she means "normal."

By "scary," she means "Indian."

By "scary," she means "Choctaw."

Choctaw, isn't it, how one narrative bleeds into another... and so it goes with *Choctalking On Other Realities*. One memory leads to another memory, which leads to an observation, which leads to a family story, which leads to a comical encounter overseas, which illuminates a Choctaw mode of being in the world, which leads to yet another observation about Oklahoma, which prompts another memory, and the narrative spins on, always turning on the axis of Choctaw history and culture. In this extraordinary collection, LeAnne Howe does for Choctaw storytelling what *The Hunger Games* does for archery—makes something seemingly traditional and archaic feel edgy, new, and necessary.

Acknowledging LeAnne's acknowledgment of her narrative tendencies feels necessary as well, as it points to an important self-awareness in her prose. A reader not familiar with her work or that of a similar writer, like Leslie Marmon Silko or Sherman Alexie, might find herself confused by the humorous but jarring leaps from, say, Choctaw tribal history to modern airline travel, to being taken hostage on a bus, to her work as a day trader, to chocolate cow patties. But, as she proves in these pages, everything is everything, which is to say that everything can or does or will lead into everything else. The route, then, from Reagan to Pearl Harbor to Japanese china goes beyond Howe's internal map of migration and memory; it's a metaphor for the connectedness among appearing disconnects.

Disconnect, as it happens, emerges as one of the great themes of this book. There is the obvious (and occasionally painful) cultural disconnect the author experiences when dealing with non-Indians. In "Carlos Castaneda Lives in Romania," our intrepid author tries to find new ways to respond to a barrage of disappointed Romanians when they learn the Choctaw are not the Yaqui and do not have a shaman like the great "Indian" Carlos Castaneda. Here, LeAnne is punished for not being Indian enough or for being the wrong kind of Indian, but on the other end of the spectrum, on a book tour in Ft. Wayne, Indiana, the author is punished for her Indianness. In "How I Lost Ten Pounds," LeAnne recounts a bizarre scene at a bookstore when a woman accosts the author because the Choctaw did not intervene in the famous 1791 battle between the Miami and the United States Army. The woman, a descendent of the general in charge of the U.S. forces, demanded an explanation for the Indian attack and justification for the lack of Choctaw intervention. LeAnne's response was (unusually) diplomatic and gracious. Nevertheless, the woman insults LeAnne and storms out of the bookstore.

Many writers would take this opportunity to wade into the self-satisfying waters of aggrievement, but LeAnne opts for a different approach. For her, these odd moments of misunderstanding, of painful racial ignorance, elicit not anger, not reproach, but humor. It seems to me it would be easier, and perhaps even cathartic, to empty the quiver here. And, to a certain degree, I suspect that is what many readers want. But, in typical Howe style, she frustrates. She trades easy antagonism for a kind of wry bemusement.

This is a remarkable choice.

It is also an aesthetic choice. Or at the very least a writerly one. When an author addresses issues of race and gender, the fall back position tends to focus on injustice, which is both appropriate and necessary. Which is why it is even more astonishing how rarely the voice in these pieces goes to that place. Rather than complain, the voice sustains. The voice does not cry or scream. It laughs, or chuckles, or sighs.

Much of the humor in these pieces arises out of the gaps between what people imagine about Indians, what popular culture tells them Indians are, and what they do when confronted with LeAnne. That is a perfect storm of kerfuffle. Things don't mesh. Worlds collide. Defensiveness emerges. But not on LeAnne's part. In this way, she reminds me of our fellow Oklahoman, Will Rogers, who was one of the best when it came to using humor as a dagger. His ability to cut to the core of a social or political issue was legendary. He was pithy and insightful. Being funny just made him that much more effective. One of Rogers's most famous quotes—"Everybody is ignorant, only on different subjects"—could be the epigraph for this very book.

Interestingly, LeAnne is hardest on herself. We never really see her lose her composure in *this* country with our own boneheads; we only see her come unmoored when she is culturally unmoored, as in Japan. "I Fuck Up In Japan" is probably my favorite piece in the book, in part because we get to see LeAnne doing to her Japanese hosts what has been done to her for a good bit of her life. She is culturally unaware and more than once culturally insensitive. If you travel across country with her, you'll quickly discover those sets of behaviors are not reserved for the Japanese, but that's a different story. In Japan, she finds herself unintentionally dissing her gracious, deferential host *and* a gigantic Buddha, along with the sacred space they all occupy. All of a sudden, *LeAnne Howe,* not some clueless Anglo, is the one committing the faux pas. It is a fantastic moment. The degree to which we are all connected and at the same time disconnected emerges here in the most fascinating ways, and it suggests that, at least tangentially, LeAnne is connected to the still-bitter descendant of General St. Clair. We all have our conflict points. We all are defensive about something. However, having those points and being brave enough to write about them are two different things.

Phillip Lopate has said that when someone writes a memoir or an autobiographical essay, the author enters into a silent bargain with the reader. That bargain is this: you give me your time and attention, and I will give you candor. Readers don't always come out on the best end of that deal, but in the case of *Choctalking,* I think they do. People who tell LeAnne that Indians don't pay taxes are easy targets. But, the self is the slipperiest, hardest target of all. It's constantly moving, and it really does not want an arrow driven into its core. So, it takes a certain level of courage—especially for a Native woman—to write about her own cultural missteps. Like Rogers, LeAnne turns potentially tense situations into self-effacing moments of insight. Each essay, each story features mini-epiphany after mini-epiphany.

Both LeAnne and Aunt Lute Books frame this collection as (at least in part) a travel book, which is accurate on a number of levels. The pieces here explore what happens when LeAnne travels both domestically and internationally. Her essays on Japan, Jordan, and Romania provide a truly unique reading experience—and I would say birth a new genre: the American Indian Abroad Narrative. There is so little Native American travel writing out there, and yet no genre seems more interesting. It is only after we are fully immersed in the stories do we realize how rare it is to see other countries from the perspective of an American Indian. So much Native writing is about America vs.

Native America, but in these revelatory essays, LeAnne takes
Native American Writing global, and the results should make
the literary community take note.

Of course, the sassy Indian abroad tales might appear to
be sexier, but her smart narratives about her book tours here in
California and in the Heartland are, to me, even more poignant
because of unexpected overlap in the International and Domestic
LeAnne Howe Venn Diagram. Whether she's writing about
driving from Jordan to Beirut for dinner or being dumped at a
fire station by a hopped up grandma outside Sacramento, LeAnne
is always trying to figure out one thing—who we are. For me, who
we are goes beyond code concepts like "identity." Sure, identity is
in there, but one of the discoveries both LeAnne and her readers
make is that who we are transcends (or at least extends beyond)
mere identity politics. In a world increasingly obsessed with
difference, this book suggests a refreshing shared goofiness.

Like her fabulous 2001 novel *Shell Shaker* and her equally
fabulous follow-up, *Miko Kings* (2007), *Choctalking* also travels
across time. In this case the historical period covered is LeAnne's
own life. The earliest piece in the book, "Moccasins Don't Have
High Heels" (which was the first thing I ever read by her), was
written in 1991. The most recent pieces, "Carlos Castaneda Lives
in Romania," "Yaa Jordan, Yaa 'Ayouni," and "Embodied Tribalography," though started in 2012, were all finished in 2013. In
other words, this book serves as an autobiographical sideshow of
twenty-two years of LeAnne Howe's writing life. Watch her write
her way through the 90s! See her navigate the 2000s! The 2010s
might be a tad rocky—will she make it? Time and place(s) are
LeAnne's great themes, as well as how ethically or unethically we
make our way through both. In her fiction, we get to be voyeurs
and observe her characters (some more Howe-esque than
others) navigate the dangerous waters of both place and time.
But here, the character—and I do mean character—is LeAnne
herself. And there seems to be more at stake in the journey,
more risked in all modes of travel.

Choctalking is a travel narrative in a formal sense as well. I
urge the reader to pay attention to how Howe travels from story

to story, from time period to time period, and from genre to genre. This is a book on the move. The narratives are themselves little voyages, and are even voyages within voyages. Almost nothing is linear; nothing moves in a straight line, follows a direct course, or travels a straight road. LeAnne likes going off the narrative grid. She likes four-wheeling. Imagine her essays are the streets of Amman, and let yourself get lost. If we think of travel as a journey, as a mode of exploration, then we can think of the pieces collected here and the voice(s) connecting them as journeying stories.

I want to talk briefly about humor, in part because it allows me to bring up Will Rogers again. He was funny. LeAnne is funny. And, let's be honest: Oklahomans are funny. It's part of our cultural coding. I've worked hard to make this introduction blandly funny; its default setting is all-out hilarity. LeAnne felt no such compunction in these pieces. As I stated earlier, at almost every moment when one expects her to veer toward trauma or drama, she opts for comedy. In fact, both Howe and Rogers choose comedy over tragedy. Some might misread this tendency as a form of deflection, but I think of it more as a form of sublimation. Tragedy has a partial basis in fear, while comedy is partially based on hope. I don't know that laughter is always the best medicine; it can be a brutal weapon. But I do think that humor highlights commonalities rather than spotlights transgressions. For all of the weirdness and wrongness described in this book, it is, at its core, highly optimistic.

Some will want to read LeAnne's wit through the lens of "Indian humor," or "Indi'n humor" if you want to be extra clever. This approach makes me uncomfortable. Is LeAnne funny because she's Indian? Does this mean all Indians are funny? Are the Choctaw particularly humorous? When LeAnne cracks a joke is she performing Indianness? Choctawness? I know of no one who thinks Will Rogers is funny *because* he was Cherokee, but when it comes to contemporary literature, it seems to be easier to compartmentalize: That's *chic lit*. That's *gay*. That's *Indian*.

And yet, *not* to acknowledge the long tradition of Indian humor is equally problematic. "Humor," says the great Oklahoma writer N. Scott Momaday, "is really where the language lives, you know. It's very close to the center and very important." The history of Indian humor is much less well known than the history of Indian suffering. Let me say right here that it is time to reverse that trend. Let this book be the domino that sets things off.

Speaking of setting things off, I want to turn now to what I think is the most important concept in the book—tribalography. I believe it is the most significant theory of American Indigenous writing to emerge in the last 20 years—maybe ever. This concept makes its way into three of the essays here, and it helps bridge the gaps between the most significant approaches to American Indian Studies—nationalism, sovereignty, issues of land and place, history, and culture. In her most provocative claim, she asserts that the story of America is a tribalography, that Indians in essence help create America's Americanness. It is a theory of how everything comes to be, though localized through Indigenous points of origin, and even more specifically within tribes and communities themselves. I predict that as the field of American Indian studies grows, more and more scholars will start to use LeAnne's theory of tribalography as a point of departure for Native fiction, poetry, criticism, drama, and film. It has certainly changed how I see things; in fact, I use tribalography prominently in my book *Engaged Resistance* across genres, and I maintain I sound the smartest when I'm ventriloquizing LeAnne.

Since I've just referenced LeAnne talking, it's probably time to make a graceful exit and let you move from my voice to hers. She's way more interesting.

Dean Rader, August 2013

Prologue: My Mothers, My Uncles, Myself

My mother walked her shoes off on the bare floors of the boarding house in Edmond, Oklahoma, as she carried me in her soft round belly the final three weeks before I was born.

Auntie Mm's in Edmond was not much more than a holding pen for unwed Indians and non-Indian women in the last weeks of their pregnancies. Local church ladies would preach to the women at Auntie Mm's on why they should have remained celibate, why they should give up their babies for adoption, and that some day good men of grace and courage would come along...if only they'd accept the Lord Jesus Christ as their personal saviors.

1951 was a difficult time for a big-bellied Indian woman. Unwed and alone (her mother had died in 1948), neither my mother's sisters nor her father knew she was pregnant—or so she thought. After she came home from Edmond without a baby my grandfather said, "Even cats nurse their young." Mother said he never spoke of what she'd done again.

When she talked about that time in her life, she'd wait for a moment, clear her throat and then tell me again how the other women at Auntie Mm's felt. "Those church ladies made the white women mad," she'd remark in a low thin voice. "One older pregnant woman hollered at those church ladies. She said it was the men who put us here. Go talk to the men."

But my mother omitted how she felt. I was supposed to know. Over the years I learned the language of her silences. Belly Mother is Choctaw. A full-blood. When she knew I was coming, she went to her older brother for help, and together they found Auntie Mm's.

About this time there was a family of Cherokee women from Stonewall, Oklahoma, who wanted to adopt a baby. They heard that a famous Indian lawyer was practicing law in Seminole, so they went to see him. He began to ask around, "Is there anyone who will give a baby away?"

Although he never said so, my uncle must have heard this message floating in the air around McAlester, Oklahoma. *"Is there anyone who will give a baby away?"* My uncle contacted the Indian lawyer about his sister, the one who was swelling out of her shoes in the boarding house in Edmond.

The circumstances must have seemed natural for the Indian lawyer and my uncle. It was an old-time trade between Indian families: one had something, one wanted something. To add to the accord, my father was part Cherokee, at least that's what he told my mother the night they made me.

On April 29 at 3:26 A.M. I arrived, and my birth mother left for McAlester the day after I was born. Without me. The baby born before me was blinded when someone put the wrong solution in its eyes. With me, however, they were careful. I was lucky. I could see. My trade could be executed.

Five days later, my Cherokee mother tenderly folded her arms like a basket and carried me away from the white people and disgrace. In the photographs taken on that day, Basket Mother holds me in front of her body like a prize. And it has been in her arms I stayed. Periodically, though, I would return to lay my head against the belly of my mother, relearning old rhythms.

This is my story. This is how I came to have two mothers: Belly Mother, the one who carried me inside her, and Basket Mother, the one who carried me in front of her.

As I've thought about my identity as a Choctaw writer, it's become clearer over the years how much "everything does matter." When I write fiction, poetry, or history, I pull together the passages of my life, and the lives of my mothers, my mothers' mothers, my uncles, and the greater community of *chafachúka* ("family") and *iksa* (adopted group or "clan"), to form the basis for critique, interpretation, a moment in time. My obligation is that I must learn more about my ancestors and myself in order to create. Then I must render all our collective experiences into a meaningful form. I call this process "tribalography." Whether it is fiction, poetry, a play, or history, American Indian writers and storytellers create tribalography to inform ourselves and the non-Indian world about who we are.

I am part Cherokee on my father's side, and adopted by a Cherokee family, yet I'm wholly Choctaw. Until the twentieth century, Choctaws were matrilineal by custom and laws, meaning that we traced descent through our mother and her relatives. The French colonial records are full of discussions in the early eighteenth century on how Choctaws identified kinship: a child made belonged to its mother and her kin. The French were astonished at this cultural difference between themselves and the Choctaws, so they wrote about it. Even as late as 1906, the Choctaws were still applying tribal customs to maintain cultural identity. That year the Choctaw and Chickasaw Freedman's Association, a joint organization of non-Indians (at least as far as the tribes were concerned), argued before a committee of U.S. Senators that they were entitled to be included on the Dawes Rolls, and entitled to allotment lands just as other Choctaws and Chickasaws. They based their argument on the fact that many of their members were illegitimate descendants of Choctaw fathers and black mothers. Melvin Cornish, the attorney for both the Choctaws and Chickasaw Nations, pointed out that according to tribal customs, illegitimate children always followed the "status of the mother," meaning they were the children of their mothers. Congress used Cornish's argument as their basis for closing the Dawes Rolls to the Freedman Association members (which, conveniently, supported the government's ongoing policies to curtail Freedman cases). I'm not attempting to take sides about the Freedman issue, rather I'm suggesting that motherhood mattered in tribal customary law to both Choctaws and Chickasaws when determining who their citizens were.

My Uncles

Mothers' brothers, the uncles, have special roles in Choctaw culture that are different from European American "uncle ways." In the eighteenth-century French colonial records there are clues as to how different the role of "father" was from "uncle." Uncle was responsible for the education of his sister's children. He was also the disciplinarian, which is a little bit different from European Americans' "uncle" role. Fathers were then free to love their children and be a kind of playful Peter Pan, never having to discipline their young, especially the girls.

In my case, it is my mother's brother Schlicht Billy that helped with my adoption. When I returned to my Choctaw family and reintroduced myself as a young adult, I visited my uncle's house first, telling myself into existence like a storyteller returning from a long journey. My uncle nodded as he listened to my narrative, then sent me to my mother's house. At that time, I didn't even know how to spell "matrilineal kinship system," but after studying our history, it seems to me that our culture is not dead and gone to "acculturation hell." What I had been doing "naturally"—meaning that I identified as entirely Choctaw because my mother is Choctaw—was historically "the way we were." Today (at least on paper), our identification system is open to children whose mother *or* father is Choctaw.

When I was growing up there were no men in my life except Basket Mother's brother. At the time of my adoption in 1951, Basket Mother had a husband, but he was never really a father, and I can't remember a single word he ever said to me. The main reason, I think, is that as a small child I was very sick with scarlet fever and always in the care of women. Later, I was hospitalized with rheumatic fever, and again, always in the care of women. Soon after I recovered, my adopted father tried to kill himself. He was hospitalized for insanity and never returned to our house. He eventually died of his wounds from drinking *Drano*. As a result I grew up without a male voice in my ear.

My Mothers' Mothers

Basket Mother is an artist. When life seems to fall down around her, she paints up a beautiful sky on canvas. Her stories tend to be visual, not verbal. However, her mother, my Cherokee grandmother, taught me the power of a good story. I've wished many times that I could remember how she said what she said in Cherokee. When she spoke the language her voice resonated like the wings of hummingbirds.

"Come and eat." "Come and sit by the fire." "Let's go outside and have a smoke." "Wash your hair in rainwater."

When she wanted to tell a story she would say, "Do you hear what I hear? Listen! *Ygiea-e-e.*" I am not able to write in Cherokee or make her language come alive on paper, but I remember her voice and how she'd cock her head from side to side just like a bird.

As a child I would learn that my grandmother has a powerful spirit. One night while I was in the hospital with rheumatic fever, I overheard someone say I was dying. Later my grandmother appeared to me and said a few words I couldn't understand. Then she left. Afterwards I slowly began to recover. I have written about her visit to the hospital in many stories. I've told many versions of that event, of her spirit's visit, because it so profoundly changed my life. In the story *Indians Never Say Goodbye*, I fictionalized and combined the healing event with the story my grandmother told me of the Snake People. The voice in this story is mine, but it is my first attempt at embodying Grandmother's voice as well.

There she was standing over me. She inched her face close to my face. She put her hands on my face. I remembered her immediately, but did not speak. My eyes blurred. They were hot and heavy. It hurt to look at Ain't Sally. It hurt to see.

I closed my eyes. I felt her cool touch. She chanted. "You will be well. You will not die. *Chim achukma taha che.* You will be well. *Chi pesa taha che.*"

She sang to me before I heard her leave.

A woman whose bed was surrounded by white partitions moaned again. This was not a new sound. It was a constant. Her breath whistled irregularly. There was no escaping the whistling sounds in the white room. Then they stopped.

Before the hospital. Before rheumatic fever. Before the dead woman. I had met Ain't Sally, grandmother's great aunt. I was seven years old.

Ain't Sally was an ancient relative who lived in Hayrick, outside of Dublin. A place of the Snakes. A place of memory.

Once a base camp for nomadic tribes following buffalo, once a county seat, Hayrick, Texas, took its name from a solitary mountain standing in the breadth of open grasslands. Only a state government road sign remains, marking the place of Hayrick. Marking the sign of the Snakes.

The only time we visited Ain't Sally, I rode in the back seat of our green 1950 Chevrolet, and listened to Grandmother tell stories about our family. Chapters went like this:

-Life in a Dugout.

-Making Lye Soap.

-How Grandfather got VD.

When we arrived at Ain't Sally's, she ambled out of a paintless wooden house as if a living corpse. Breasts sagging, her thin body lacking in strength seemed unable to support her weight. Her sleeveless dress revealed dark brown skin. Hairless underarms.

She fed Grandmother and me saltine crackers and cold squirrel dumplings. Ain't Sally asked me questions about my secrets. I don't remember having any to tell. But she told me hers while I ate.

She said I reminded her of someone she'd known a long time ago. I remember dancing for her and told her I was a bird. The manbird. A hunter. I danced around her kitchen table and sang and pretended to be PowWow Dancer. A bird of dance, a bird of rhythm.

When we walked outside into the sun, a hot gusty wind picked up her voice like dust tendrils on bedrock and blew it away from me. I ran to catch the sound and found Ain't Sally sitting on a granite rock.

"Indian girl. *Alla Tek.*

"Come and see, on our land, the four winds of the old days will blow through our hair." Then she tugged at my black braids.

"Come and visit the Snakes, *Alla Tek.*

"When I was your age they blew across this place like red dust devils on flat neutral plains.

"Can you see them?

"Do you hear the Snake People calling us?"

"Yes. I can see them," I said. "I hear them. They're hungry."

I watched the Snake People eat the fleshy intestines of my uncle's butchered cow. I tasted the hot blood, rolled it around on my tongue and remembered. It made me sweat.

The Snake People played games around the carcass. And before we walked back into the house, she put her crooked fingers across my eyes and said:

"Indian Girl. *Alla Tek.*

The ghosts of your ancestors will visit you there."[1]

The Snake People in the story were Comanches. According to my grandmother, the Comanches often traveled across her great aunt's land and bargained for cows. When I learned that story I was looking across the same land that Grandmother had seen as a young girl.

Indian Women Don't Document Change; They Make Change[2]

I grew up in houses of women and the world looked pretty woman-centric to me. I had two Native mothers, both from Southeastern tribes. I also had a Cherokee grandmother who talked of spirits and medicine. My aunts had gone to Haskell Institute for high school. Two great aunts had moved to California and worked in the airplane factories in WWII. Another great aunt had joined the circus and never returned to Southeastern Oklahoma. And a great-great aunt had treated with the Comanche. As a child and young woman, it seemed to me women were in charge of everything and everyone in Southeastern Oklahoma. But life was also very complicated: I had two families, and I was often introduced as the "adopted daughter," or the "daughter that had been given away." Both my mothers could be cruel and suspicious of the separate lives I was living when I wasn't with them. And sometimes I felt ashamed at being adopted out.

I married in the late 1960s and had two sons. It was as a mother that I realized that both my mothers really never had men in their lives for long periods of time, and I seemed to be following the same pattern. By the time I was twenty-three, I was a divorced mother with two small children and had entered college. My life became more and more schizophrenic. I wanted to be a mother, a student, a lawyer, a writer, a Choctaw woman with a job in which I didn't have to say, "Can I freshen up your coffee, *hon*?"

In 1977, I started an entertainment newspaper in Fort Worth, Texas called *Worth Magazine* with Sheree Turner. We ran the business, wrote poetry, and covered rock concerts at Tarrant County Convention Center. During these years I was writing fiction. In the early 1980s, most of the Native fiction being published was about Indians-on-the-rez and events that happened to Plains Indians. This left *me*, as a reader and writer of fiction, hungry for urban stories about Southeastern Indians. But at the time, no one wanted to hear about urban Indians who'd supposedly "lost" their culture to the city. So the late Choctaw author Roxy Gordon and I decided to write a play set in Oklahoma City among urban Indians, titled *Big PowWow*. Sojourner Truth Theater in Fort Worth, Texas produced the play in 1987. The central character, Blossom Bird Song, is a contemporary Choctaw woman with problems. She's overweight and has diabetes, chases after the wrong kind of men, and she needs a job. After an Old Ghost, *Tullock-Chish-Ko* appears to her and her social worker Brooke, Blossom decides she must change and adapt.

Big PowWow was the first collaboration in Texas that brought an all-American Indian cast together with a producer and director who are African Americans. While Sojourner Truth Theater does not think of itself as an indigenous theater company, we found that our collaboration was successful because both the American Indian cast and playwrights and the African American producer and director believed that we had a kind of social responsibility to explore our cultural heritage[s] and to render them meaningful to an audience. Something beyond stereotypes.

Women and the Word

Historically, Choctaw women were representatives of the "Word" and had roles as important as men in the tribal life, both as cultural ambassadors *and* representatives of their families and *oklas* ("people"). In the mid-eighteenth century, the French traveler and adventurer Jean-Bernard Bossu made an interesting comment concerning Choctaw women speakers. Writing in his journal he claimed that women loved their husbands so much they followed them in battle.

"Some women are so fond of their husbands that they follow them to war. They keep by their sides in combat holding a quiver of arrows and encourage them by crying out continually that they must not fear their enemies, but die like true men. So fond of the men that they tell them they must die like true men."[3]

I suggest there may have been other reasons that Choctaw women went into battle: Choctaw women spoke the words of power that could turn a battle in the tribe's favor. I wrote about the power of breath and mind in *Shell Shaker* expressed through the characters of Auda Billy, Susan Billy, and Tema Billy, and of course Shakbatina.

There are many examples of Choctaw women as ambassadors in the French colonial period. While historians have overlooked them, they are nevertheless in the documents. One such instance is contained in a letter dated February 1746 from M. de Louboey, the King's Lieutenant of Mobile, to Jean Frédéric Phelypeaux, Count de Maurepas, Minister of the Marines and the Colonies from 1723-1749. In this letter it is clear from Louboey's point of view that the peace mission succeeded *because* a Choctaw woman was involved as ambassador or giver of the "Word" in the negotiations between the French, the Choctaws, and the Chickasaws.[4]

My Choctaw birth mother's grandmother was named Anolitubbee, "tells and kills." The mantle of her name reflects the power she embodied in the community. As a storyteller she carried the words for making change, speaking away the bad and/or evil in a political situation so that good feelings could grow in its place. My adopted Cherokee grandmother also made sure that *I* would become a storyteller. In a way I am the bridge between blood and adopted kin. By birth and tradition, I'm trying to do what my ancestors wanted—tell stories. I've been writing through the events that shaped our lives, theirs and mine. In breathing life onto the page, I embody the lives of my relatives—my mothers, my mothers' mothers, and my uncles—through the stories. I leave you with a poem that speaks with the power of breath and mind.

I

Each morning, *Hashi*, the stark red creator rises, swelling,
she passes over the ground, spilling a drop or two of her blood which
grows the corn, and the people: Choctaw that is we.

Naked, she goes down on us,
Her flaming hair burns us brown.
Finally, in the month of *Tek lnhashi,* the Sun of
  Women,
when we are navel deep in red sumac, we cut the
  leaves and
smoke to her success. Sing her praises.
Hashi, Creator Sun, won't forget.

II
When *Ohoyo lkbi* pulled
freshly-made Choctaw
out of her red thighs,
we were very wet, so
one-by-one,
she stacked us
on the mound,
and *Hashi* kissed our
bodies with her morning lips
and painted our faces with afternoon fire,
and, in the month of *Hashi Hoponi,* the Sun of
  Cooking,
we were made

III
It is said that
once-a-month warriors can kill a thing with spit.
So when the soldiers came,
our mothers stood on the tops of the
ramparts and made the *tashka* call
urging their men on.
Whirling their tongues and hatchets in rhythm,
they pulled red water and fire from their bodies
and covered their chests with bullet-proof blood.
And when it was over,

they made a fire bed on the prairie that
blew across the people like a storm;
melded our souls with iron.
And in the month of *Hashi Mali,* the Sun of Wind,
we listen for the voices
that still urge us on
at sunrise[5]

Notes

1 "Indians Never Say Good-bye." *Reinventing the Enemy's Language,* 1997.

2 This is a paraphrase of something Rayna Green, director of the American Indian Program at National Museum of American History at the Smithsonian Institution, says in her article "Native American Women." (*Signs: Journal of Women in Culture and Society,* 1980, vol. 6, no. 2. The University of Chicago).

3 Jean-Bernard Bossu's *Travels in the Interior of North America,* 1751-1762, Norman: University of Oklahoma Press, 1962, p. 163.

4 *Mississippi Provincial Archives: French Dominion, 1729-1748, Vol. IV,* Rowland, Sanders, and Galloway, Louisiana State University Press, 1984, p. 260.

5 *Gatherings: The Enowkin Journal of First North American Peoples,* Vol. IV—1993.

The Story of America
A Tribalography

It doesn't end.

In all growing
from all earths
to all skies,

in all touching
all things,

in all soothing
the aches of all years,
it doesn't end.

(Simon Ortiz, "It Doesn't End, Of Course," 1976: 147)

Native stories are power. They create people. They author tribes. America is a tribal creation story, a tribalography.

As numerous as Indian tribes, creation stories gave birth to our people, and it is with absolute certainty that I tell you now—our stories also created the immigrants who landed on our shores. I don't mean that native people imagined them as their God did, nor "formed man of the dust of the ground, and breathed into his nostrils the breath of life" (Genesis 2: 8). But our stories made the immigrants Americans nevertheless.

When the foreigners arrived and attempted to settle in the upper Northeast, they had nothing to eat, nothing to sustain them but their faith in biblical stories. Indigenous people told them new stories of how to live in our world. One example of this is the native story of the Three Sisters (Beauchamp 1897: 177). Natives told stories of how to plant their crops, corn, beans, and pumpkins (squash), which sustained the newcomers and taught them how to experiment with their daily diet by adding variety. As a result, native foods were traded internationally and changed the food cultures of the entire world. According to the National Corn Growers Association's January 2000 statistics, corn is grown in more countries in the world than any other crop, and the United States produces and exports more corn than any other country in the world. In 2011, according to the National Corn Growers Association website, http://www.ncga.com/, corn represents 76.62 billion dollars in crop value compared with wheat at 35.76 billion. Worldwide corn production still leads all other grains. Currently products made from corn include everything from sweeteners, distillers, ethanol, corn oil, crayons, and fabrics made from cornstarch. Maize was developed from Teosinte, a wild grass that was growing in Central Mexico as early as 7,000 years ago and propagated by Native plant scientists some 4,000 years ago in the Western Hemisphere, although there is disagreement on how corn spread into North America. Thanksgiving is the holiday in which Americans give thanks to indigenous people for such extraordinary and versatile foods. But the most important story the immigrants would hear from Natives was how to make a united nation by combining people from various tribes. It is this eloquent act of unification that explains how America was created from a story, hence my title: "The Story of America: A Tribalography."

Before I continue with the scholarly account of tribalog-raphy, I want to tell you a Choctaw story. My tribe's language has a mysterious prefix that, when combined with other words, represents a form of creation. It is *nuk* or *nok*, and it has to do with the power of speech, breath, and mind. Things with *nok* or *nuk* attached to them are so powerful they create. For instance, *nukfokechi* brings forth knowledge and inspiration. A teacher is a *nukfoki*, the beginning of action. *Nuklibisha* is to be in a state of passion, and *nukficholi* means to hiccup, or breath that comes out accidentally.

My story begins in September. I was standing on the front porch of my house in Iowa City, Iowa. The sky was bright blue; there was no wind. Rabbits and ghosts of rabbits hopped in the front yard, playing tag with a couple of gray squirrels. After a time I looked at the southern sky and saw what appeared to be black specks of pepper floating in the upper atmosphere. As they glided closer to the earth, I realized they were red-tailed hawks. There were so many I couldn't believe they really were hawks, so I ran into the house and found my binoculars. One, four, seven, twenty-two. Eventually, there were forty-four hawks kettling together, heading for the Iowa River valley. As the first group disappeared, another group of hawks flew into view, their red tail feathers reflecting the mid-morning sunlight. Over the next thirty minutes, dozens more appeared.

Red-tailed hawks are very special to Choctaw people. They can weigh up to ten pounds and their body feathers are variegated browns and whites, but their tail feathers are a bright reddish-orange, the color of fire. As I stood in the middle of my yard, their numbers began to dwindle until there were only fours, sevens; then it happened. One red-tailed hawk flew right over my head and landed in a tree about thirty yards from my porch. He perched on a broken branch and appeared to be looking in my direction. We regarded one another for a while and it was then that I realized my Grandmother was trying to tell me something: the hawks have returned.

Grandmother was a storyteller and she taught me the power of story. When I was growing up she was the one who told stories late into the night. Sometimes she'd say, "Do you hear what I hear? Listen! *Ygiea-e-e.*" Then she would begin a story.

"I don't know if you remember old Lum Jones," she'd say, cocking her head in my direction. "One night, I was looking out my picture window when the Angel of Death walked down the sidewalk in front of my house. He went up on Lum Jones' front porch next door. Before I knew what had happened, he was carrying Lum Jones up through the tree tops," she said. "I'm telling the truth."

From her story, I could see what had happened. A large man-bird first showed himself to her by gliding past her house. Then he slipped soundlessly inside the walls of Lum Jones' house and carried the old man in his beak up, up, up, through the loving arms of the gigantic elm in the front yard. Together, the old man and the bird-man winged their way toward the heavens. Of course, everyone in my family agreed that right after Grandmother saw Lum Jones being carried up through the tree, he was as dead as Andrew Jackson. It was a fact. Grandmother could see life and death, and she told me not to be afraid of either one. That was the first lesson I learned from her.

Then one night while I was in the hospital with rheumatic fever, I overheard someone saying that I was going to die. I had had a lot of heart problems, so in a way I was not surprised, but I was afraid of leaving my family. Later my Grandmother appeared to me, first, as a huge brown hawk about the size of a person hovering over my bed. I knew it was my grandmother because the bird had a beak shaped like her nose. In the next moment, Grandmother was standing next to me with her hand on my forehead. She had transformed herself from a winged person back into a human person. She said a few words I couldn't understand, then she left. After a long while, I gradually got well. Much later, Grandmother explained that she was the one who visited me as a bird. She said she would always watch over me.

When Grandmother ended a story, she'd squeal in her high-pitched old-lady voice: "Whee-e-e that's enough, I can tell you no more today." Then she'd whistle at the canaries and parakeets she kept on her back porch. Then she'd have a smoke.

There were always many varieties of birds around my Grandmother's house and she worried constantly that their numbers were becoming thin. She told me that when she was growing up at the turn of the century dozens of hawks and eagles visited her house. She said that back in the old days it wasn't unusual to see them everywhere, but that wasn't the case in the early 1960s. Hunters had killed a lot of game birds, hawks, and eagles, during the first half of the century. Then, farmers had sprayed pesticides that ended up killing all her favorite songbirds.

Right before my Grandmother died, she said the birds never stopped talking to her, telling her stories. She said that they kept her up all night, making her ears ring, and it was their music that she died listening to, not our voices.

To some who read this story, it may seem like a family memoir. I loved my Grandmother and she loved me. And birds. But American and British behavioral scientists have shown that birds have been found to have the same kind of memory that enables people to recall where they left their house keys. A study published in *Nature* (September 17, 1998) marks what researchers say is the *first* demonstration of episodic, or event-based memory in animals other than humans. Two researchers, Nicola S. Clayton and Anthony Dickinson, (1998: 272) have shown that birds have memories much the same as humans.

The recollection of past experiences allows us to recall what a particular event was, and where and when it occurred, a form of memory that is thought to be unique to humans. It is known, however, that food-storing birds remember the spatial location and contents of their caches. Furthermore, food-storing animals adapt their caching and recovery strategies to the perish-ability of food stores, which suggest that they are sensitive to temporal factors. (Clayton and Dickinson 1998: 272)

So birds, like people (who bring their favorite snacks to eat while watching a Saturday afternoon football game on television) can remember not only when and where but also what kind of food they've stored for the future.

This is big news to white people, or people educated in mainstream institutions, but not to American Indians who have been telling stories of birds as creators, birds as tricksters, birds as healers, and birds with long memories. At last it seems another group of storytellers, the scientists, have now "proven" that birds demonstrate they too, have episodic, or event-based, memories.

I tell the story about my grandmother because it is a good example of what I am trying to address: the power of Native stories. First, there was the event, the birds, then Grandmother's story and her transformation into a bird, her life and death, and the re-appearance of red-tailed hawks. The story I am telling you now is *nukfokechi*. It brings forth knowledge and inspires us to make the eventful leap that one thing leads to another.

Choctaws have many stories about birds. One story says that a long time ago there came to the Choctaws an Unknown Woman. While it is the story about how the Unknown Woman brought corn to the people, it also incorporates birds and their relationship to people. The woman is a stranger who appears in the moonlight atop a great hill. Two hunters see her as if in a vision:

> Happening to look behind them in the direction opposite the moon they (two hunters) saw a woman of wonderful beauty standing upon a mound a few rods distant. Like an illuminating shadow, she had suddenly appeared out of the moon-lighted forest. She was loosely clad in a snow-white raiment, and bore in the folds of her drapery a wreath of fragrant flowers. She beckoned them to approach, while she seemed surrounded by a halo of light that gave to her a supernatural appearance. Their imagination now influenced them to believe her to be the Great Spirit of their nation, and that the flowers she bore were representatives of loved ones who had passed from

Earth to bloom in the Spirit-Land. (Cushman 1899: 277)

The Unknown Woman tells the two men that she's hungry, and they offer her roasted hawk meat. This special meat of the hawk is all they have, so they give it willingly. The woman eats only a small bite, then tells them to return the following mid-summer at the same place atop the mound. She promises she'll be there. The next year, at exactly the same time, the two hunters return and find corn growing atop the mound. From the hunters' initial gift of sacred food to the Unknown Woman, Choctaws and other southeastern tribes received the gift of corn. Today we celebrate Green Corn Ceremony in mid-summer to mark the coming of the future: corn, our ancient food cache. Another version of this story explains how a black bird brought corn, *tanchi*, to a Choctaw boy.

Everything is Everything

"Everything exists and everything will happen and everything is alive and everything is planned and everything is a mystery, and everything is dangerous, and everything is a mirage, and everything touches everything, and everything is everything, and everything is very, very strange." This quote is from a painting by the late Roxy Gordon, painted in 1988. An author and artist, Gordon evokes, in a very Choctaw way, the basic principles of Lynn Margulis' scientific theory on symbiogenesis which says that the merger of previously independent organisms is of great importance to evolutionary change. Margulis is renown internationally as a biologist for her research on the evolution of eukaryotic cells—cells with a nucleus. As professor in the department of geosciences at the University of Massachusetts at Amherst she was awarded in March 2000, along with eleven others, the National Medal of Science by President Clinton. She has chaired the National Academy of Science's Space Science Board Committee on Planetary Biology and Chemical Evolution that aided in the development of research strategies for NASA, and in 1981, she received a NASA Public Service award. She has written many books on scientific topics, both for children and adults, including *What is Life? Essays in Gaia, Symbiosis, and Evolution,* and *Microcosmos: Four Billion Years of Evolution from Our Microbial Ancestors* (co-authored with science collaborator and son, Dorian Sagan).

The story of how a human—a being made of nucleated cells—evolves from an ameboid being—a nucleated cell—is bizarre. But even this story has a preamble: the evolution of a cell with a nucleus. How did such a cell evolve?

The quick answer is by the merging of different kinds of bacteria. Protoctists evolved through symbiosis; twigs and limbs on the tree of life not only branched out but grew together and fused. Symbiosis refers to an ecological and physical relationship between two kinds of organisms that is far more intimate than most associations. In Africa, for example, plovers pluck and eat leeches from the open mouths of crocodiles without fear. Bird and beast in this instance are behavioral symbionts; crocodiles enjoy clean teeth in the company of well-fed plovers. Bacteria live in the spaces between our teeth and in our intestines, mites inhabit our eyelashes; all these tiny beings draw nutriment from our cells or our uneaten food, as cells are shed or as they excrete organic excess. Symbiosis, like marriage, means living together for better or worse; but whereas marriage is between two different people, symbiosis is between two or more different types of live beings. (Margulis and Sagan, 1995: 96)

In other words, biologists like Margulis have adopted a Choctawan way of looking at the world. "Everything touches everything, and everything is everything," as Gordon phrased it. The theory of symbiosis advanced by Margulis and her colleagues also suggests that evolution is the result of cooperation, not simply competition:

Next the view of evolution as chronic bloody competition among individuals and species, a popular distortion of Darwin's notion of "survival of the fittest," dissolves before a new view of continual cooperation, strong interaction, and mutual dependence among life forms. Life did not take over the globe by combat, but by networking. Life forms multiplied and complexified by co-opting others, not just by killing them. (Margulis and Sagan, 1986:14)

Much like the Choctaw prefix *nuk* that when combined with other words it represents a form of creation, Lynn Margulis' scientific theory is also *nukfokechi*.

Consider another storyteller, Pisatuntema, a Choctaw woman who in 1909 told the story of the hunter who became a deer. Her story shows what Margulis and Sagan say that life does. One thing *combines* with another thing to form "life" the verb, a process that is always in flux:

One night, a hunter killed a doe and soon afterward fell asleep near the carcass. The next morning, just at sunrise, the hunter was surprised and startled to see the doe raise her head and to hear her speak, asking him to go with her to her home. At first he was so surprised that he did not know what to reply, so the doe again asked him whether he would go. Then the hunter said that he would go with her, although he had no idea where she would lead him...[Ed]. Now all around the cave were piles of deer's feet, antlers, and skins. While the hunter was asleep the deer endeavored to fit to his hands and feet deer's feet which they selected for the purpose. After several unsuccessful attempts the fourth set proved to be just the right size and were fastened firmly on the hunter's hands and feet. Then a skin was found that covered him properly, and finally antlers were fitted to his head. And then the hunter became a deer and walked on four feet after the manner of deer. (Bushnell 1909: 32)

There are Choctaws, including myself, who consider Pisatuntema's story a biology lesson about creating kin with people
and things who are different from ourselves. But there are many
possibilities in this story. When all the tribes in the Southeast
began to hunt deer to near extinction in the eighteenth century, a
relationship evolved between Indian hunter, deer, and foreigner.
This event is what historians have called "the deerskin trade." As
scholar Kathryn E. Holland Braund has noted, "Trade is a mutual
affair" (Braund 1993: xiii). This does not mean that all sides
are equal, but rather all sides have agency and are networking.
"Between 1699 and 1705, Carolina shipped an average of over
forty-five thousand deerskins annually to London. And between
1705 and 1715, the trade in deerskins was the most valuable
business endeavor in the colony" (Braund 1993: 29). She goes on
to explain that Indian trading companies forged links to Creek
Chickasaw and Choctaw towns, "about one hundred thousand
Weight of Skins were shipped from Augusta in 1741" (Braund
1993: 97). Another event, however, occurs among the Choctaw.
In the town of Chickasawhay, a large Choctaw community of the
eighteenth century, hunters forgo the hunting season of 1764.
Historian Richard White suggests that the reason they did this
was because deer were becoming scarce. "That the town suffered
from a depletion of deer is also suggested by its reputation as a
collection of stock thieves and later, more positively, as a center
of stock raising in the nation" (White 1983: 86). But stories make
connections. Choctaws would have been sensitive to the fact
that they were the cause of the scarcity of deer, a source of food.
A story of what may happen if the cycle continues seems to hold
creative solutions.

Pisatuntema's story explains that the deer are fighting back.
Not only does the doe talk, but she lures the hunter into the
underground and transforms him. Only through the intervention of the hunter's mother is the hunter's blood returned to
the earth and a ceremonial dance is held. In the early Choctaw
worldview, not being returned to the earth by a bone picking

ceremony would be a kind of heresy. I wrote "Danse d'Amour, Danse De Mort" (Howe 1993: 447-472) about Choctaw bone picking and what it meant to the people in my story of the eighteenth century who saw their bodies as food for the animals and earth once they were dead. "Tchatak, the consumer. The animal, the consumed. Tchatak, the consumed. The animal the consumer" (Howe 1993: 469). Things are made right when we are returned to the earth as food for the planet. Life continues.

Choctaws have another story to explain a relationship between hunters and deer that also speaks to Margulis' theory of symbiosis. *Kashehotep*, half man, half deer, is a character who will harass hunters if they come too close to his camp where many other animals live. I suggest that people tell this story to explain what we have learned about the onslaught of ecological disasters caused by the deerskin trade of the eighteenth and nineteenth centuries.

For early scholars who studied American Indian stories, and specifically Choctaw stories, the hunter and the doe narrative has been relegated to folklore or myth, a fiction. This troubles many American Indians. Miwok author Greg Sarris, in an interview for the 1994 film series, *The Native Americans,* produced by TBS Productions, Inc., explains the prejudice inherent in the belief that Native stories are fictions:

> A team of geologists happened to be working in the creek over here and they unearthed whale fossils from the period of the last Pliocene. And we said, according to the stories that during the time of the flood that there was a whale in that creek. This was told from generation to generation for 10,000 years. They got very interested, these geologists, they said, 'these Indians have this myth that there's this whale in the creek and we found the fossils.' The Indians also say that during the time of the flood that people went on top of that mountain and went into a cave. Well, they went up to the cave and carbon-dated charcoal on the walls from fire that dated to the same period. If that's a myth, you give me some evidence of Noah's

Ark. Do you have any splinters or wood from that?
(Sarris 1994)

In the case of the whale story, bones were found to support the Indians' story. Sarris is not arguing about the Biblical flood or whether Noah's ark existed, rather he and other Natives in the film point out that no matter what physical evidence Indians have, our stories are thought to be myth.

By this time, you may be asking yourself how my boastful opening remark that America is a tribal creation story relates to Margulis' theory of symbiosis. She suggests that the merger of previously independent organisms, or systems (for the purposes of my article) is of great importance to evolutionary change. I am suggesting that when the European Founding Fathers heard the stories of how the Haudenosaunee unified six individual tribes into an Indian confederacy, they created a document, the US Constitution that united immigrant Europeans into a symbiotic union called America.

From An Indigenous Story the Europeans and Indians Unite

...It is that, therefore, that in ancient times it thus
came to pass that the hodiyaanehshon, *the Federal
Chiefs*, our grandsires, made a formal rule saying,
"Let us unite our affairs; let us formulate
regulations."
(Bierhorst 1974: 145)

The above is an excerpted quote from Iroquoian into English of an archaic translation of the "Ritual of Condolence," a portion of what is also called the Condolence ceremony. This Iroquois version of the oral drama is spoken by elders and is designed to heal the community and make it a peaceful whole. As John Bierhorst notes in *Four Masterworks*, the ritual drama was the Iroquois attempt to achieve peace between differing tribes and thwart the cult of death and warfare by forming a confederacy (Bierhorst 1974: 109-111). The Iroquois Confederacy at the time of contact with the immigrants was scattered over eastern North

America and across the contemporary US-Canadian border. They occupied most of what is now New York State, parts of neighboring Pennsylvania, and sections of Ontario and Quebec. When the immigrants settled among them and wanted to create trading networks, the Iroquois told them stories of how their ancestors had learned to live peacefully together—their story would serve as a kind of cultural template for the New World. There are many versions of the story and what follows is not a direct quote but paraphrased from a variety of sources including Onondaga elder Oren Lyons' speech at the 1987 conference at Cornell University's American Indian Program and from his interview in the 1994 six-part film series *The Native Americans*.

A long time ago there was a blood lust among the people. A great war engulfed the land and the people were full of merciless killing and fighting one another for supreme rule. Nations, towns, families were destroyed and scattered to the four winds. It was proof of the tyranny which people at that time were capable of. Then along came a great visionary leader, Degenawidah, who realized the killing must stop. He began a journey to establish peace, but he knew he had a serious handicap. He stuttered. Since storytelling is an oral art, Degenawidah knew he had to find someone who could speak for him. Along his journey he met the powerful warrior, named Ayonwatha, or Hiawatha as his name is pronounced in English. Ayonwatha, Onondaga by birth and Mohawk by adoption, was mourning the murder of his wife and children. He had vowed to wipe out his enemies, including the man he saw standing before him. But he knew Degenawidah had combed the snakes out of a powerful wizard's hair, taking away the wizard's anger, so Ayonwatha decided to go with him. Together the two men traveled throughout the land to establish peace. Through Ayonwatha's mighty gift of oratory, Degenawidah proposed that the warring tribes of the upper northeast form a confederacy.

Degenawidah became known as the Peacemaker. He set up the families into clans, and then he set up the leaders of the clans.

He established a confederacy wherein each clan would have a clanmother, and political roles for men and women would be in balance. He made two houses within each nation. One he called the Long House and the other, the Mud House. These two houses would work together in ceremony and council, establishing the inner source of vitality of their nations. The Peacemaker also made two houses in the Grand Council, one called the Younger Brothers, consisting of the Oneida, and the Cayuga Nations, and later (1715) enlarging to include the Tuscarora. The other was the Elder Brothers consisting of the Mohawks, keepers of the Eastern Door; the Onondaga, the Firekeepers; and the Senecas, keepers of the Western Door. Then Degenawidah named the united nations Haudenosaunee: The People of the Long House.

The Haudenosaunee's story remains consistent. The confederacy was founded on the core values the Peacemaker proposed: freedom, respect, tolerance, consensus, and brotherhood. Under the terms and spirit of the *NeGayane-shogowa* or the Great Law of Peace, all parties pledged themselves to the confederacy's body of laws. United we thrive, divided we fall.

After hearing the Haudenosaunee spokesmen extol the values of unification for over a hundred years, the colonists finally transformed themselves into thirteen united states and eventually wrote a document to celebrate the event, the US Constitution. As historian Robert W. Venables says, "the Haudenosaunee influenced both directly and indirectly the generation of the Founding Fathers and their various efforts to achieve unity" (Venables 1992: 68). The power and persistence of a native story convinced the separate peoples of the Old World to merge in their new homeland for their mutual benefit.

Modern scholarly stories place the formation of the Haudenosaunee, the original event, sometime around AD 1500 (Ruoff 1990: 23). Under these terms a Haudenosaunee governance known as the Council of Fifty was created and this system gave all Five Nations equal status, and was later called the Six Nations when the Tuscaroras were included in 1715. Ever since, the Six Nations have gathered to resolve their differences through common consent.

Historian Donald A. Grinde, Jr., says that numerous colonial documents exist to support the Iroquois story and its effect on the immigrants: "There is ample scholarly opinion and factual data to conclude that the Founding Fathers respected and used American Indian ideas as the American government evolved" (Grinde 1992: 47). Grinde points out that Indian confederacies were so appealing to William Penn that he described the whole of Eastern America as political societies with sachemships inherited through the female side. "Penn was also familiar with the Condolence Ceremony of the Iroquois which was crucial for an understanding of their confederacy"(Grinde 1992: 49). Again, the ceremony was an oral drama, a story, that the colonists observed. The story was about the unification of the Iroquois, and their aim was to achieve peace and unity.

It's important to remember that the influence the Haudeno-saunee had on men like William Penn was derived from Penn's firsthand knowledge of their discourse. In the case of the Haude-nosaunee, they made wampum belts to record events, but never made written accounts. Rather, their spokesmen were trained to speak and tell stories. Anthropologist Stephen A. Tyler says that "discourse is the maker of the world, not its mirror...The world is what we say it is and what we speak of is the world" (Tyler 1987: 171). Tribal spokesmen used allegory, metaphor, imagination, and inventiveness, all the techniques of storytell-ing to make their demands come true.

In the case of the Haudenosaunee, their story was about unity. Although the struggle for immigrant dominance was tumultuous, the Haudenosaunee's call for unity in the Northeast remained steady, and it is little wonder why. In the seventeenth century the Haudenosaunee had to negotiate with seven white colonial governments on the Hudson. "The inter-colonial context was equally stormy. The Haudenosaunee had to deal with New England colonies to their east and the English colonies to the south, which were rivals of the Dutch. After an English government replaced the Dutch in 1664, all the Haudenosaunee white neighbors, except the French in Canada, were now under English rule from London" (Venables 1992: 72).

In the summer of 1677, Haudenosaunee spokesmen such as Carachkondie and Connondocgoo joined with English officials from New York, Maryland, and Virginia to speak for a unified colonial policy. The Indians wanted to create a foreign policy with the English in order to cement their trade relationship with them (Venables 1992: 72). The Haudenosaunee were major political and economic partners of the English in what is now known as the Covenant Chain. Because the Indians were a counterbalance to French interest in Canada (and key to the English colonists' survival) they often used the councils to retell their origin stories and renew the Covenant Chain. This oratory benefited the Haudenosaunee in two ways. First, it presented a unified Indian image to the colonists. Second, the act of storytelling inculcates what historian Raymond D. Fogelson (1989:143) calls an epitomizing event for both speaker and listener. Whether the event in question ever happened matters very little to the people who believe it. Therefore, story creates culture and beliefs, the very glue which binds a society together.

In the western intellectual tradition, the act of writing stories (creating "documents") has been given hegemony over the act of telling stories. This phenomenon led to a privileged view of text, so much so that written stories of the past became labeled as "history," and their storytellers "historians." Currently, debate persists among anthropologists, ethno-historians, and the literary critics on what distinguishes story from history or ethnography. Anthropologist James Clifford has said in his introduction of *Writing Culture* that much of what is being written about a particular cultures is "true fiction:"

> Ethnographic writings can properly be called
> fictions in the sense of "something made or fashioned,"
> the principal burden of the word's Latin foot, *fingere*.
> But it is important to preserve the meaning not merely
> of making, but also of making up, of inventing things
> not actually real. (*Fingere*, in some of its uses, implied
> a degree of falsehood.) Interpretative social scientists
> have recently come to view good ethnographies as
> "true fictions," but usually at the cost of weakening
> the oxymoron, reducing it to the banal claim that all
> truths are constructed. (Clifford 1986: 6)

What Clifford and others are saying is that a particular text
within a discipline is not false, but always interpretive, and
most importantly, the storyteller can never undertake to tell
the whole story. The histories of Indian and white relations are
replete with documents of how Indians influenced Europeans
to unite, but the story remains only partially told. For example,
on June 24, 1744, in Lancaster, Pennsylvania, Canasatego, a
Haudenosaunee spokesman, gave his first speech on the history
of the Covenant Chain and its success in creating symbiotic
trade relationships. His manipulation of the image of Indian
hegemony in the region was considerable. Canasatego's speech
was translated by interpreter Conrad Weiser. In his concluding
remarks given on July 4, 1744, Canasatego repeated the origin
story of the Haudenosaunee (Venables 1992: 76-81). "Benjamin
Franklin printed Canasatego's speech as part of the full
record of the 1744 Lancaster negotiations. Franklin sent three
hundred copies to London to sell" (Venables 1992: 81). Canasatego's story was read by Londoners as well as colonists.

In 1754, Franklin made a proposal called the Albany Plan
to unite the colonies. On June 11, 1776, twenty-two years later,
Franklin's revised Albany Plan was given to the committee of the
Continental Congress. That group later drafted the Articles of
Confederation. James Wilson, a delegate from Pennsylvania and
future author of the first draft of the US Constitution, argued
vigorously for a confederation that was *similar* to the Haude-

nosaunee. He declared "Indians know the striking benefits of confederation...[and we] have an example of it in the Union of the Six Nations" (Ford 1904-5: 1078).

In reading the papers, memoirs, and diaries of influential colonists such as historian Cadwallader Colden, Acting Governor of New York James DeLancey, Founding Fathers Benjamin Franklin, James Madison, Thomas Jefferson, and James Wilson, as well as philosopher John Locke, it is clear that they noted the social and political effects the Indians had on them. However, what is most important to Onondaga elder Oren Lyons is that his community's story remains constant. Haudenosaunee existence predates contact with Europeans. "This is no small achievement," he says. "We have faced off with the white man for three hundred years and right from the beginning he has learned much from us. He just doesn't want to admit it" (Lyons 1994).

I include this long discussion of the Haudenosaunee story, and the early colonial writings, not because I want to enter the debate on whether the US Constitution exactly replicates Haudenosaunee governance. The Constitution, although a kind of nationalist creation story, does not in intent or function imitate Indian governance. Rather, it is my intention to argue that the Haudenosaunee's *story of their union* created an image so powerful in the minds of colonists that they believed if "savages" could unite, they ought to be able to do the same thing. That united image remained indelible in the minds of immigrants, so much so that Indians will forever be spoken of as *one group*. Today, it comes as a surprise to college students that there are still over five hundred federally-recognized tribes, each with distinct cultural practices.

What I suggest is that a native creation story was one of America's authors. If not acknowledged in the "historical credits," American Indians are certainly the ghost writers for the event, the story of America. So far, I have consciously used "story," "history," "theory" as interchangeable words because the difference in their usage is artificially constructed to privilege writing over speaking. All histories are stories that are written down. The story you get depends on the point of view of the writer. At some point histories are contextualized as "fact," a theoretically loaded word. Facts change, but stories continually bring us into being.

What is Tribalography?

> I add my breath to your breath
> That our days may be long on the Earth
> That the days of our people may be long
> That we may be one person
> That we may finish our roads together
> May our mother bless you with life
> May our Life Paths be fulfilled.
>
> (Allen 1986: 56)

Now I have come to the place where I must tell you what my term "tribalography" means, and how it achieves a new understanding in theorizing on Native and indigenous studies. This is a tall order for a storyteller, but here goes. Native stories, no matter what form they take (novel, poem, drama, memoir, film, history) seem to pull all the elements together of the storyteller's tribe, meaning the people, the land, multiple characters and all their manifestations and revelations, and connect these in past, present, and future milieu. (Present, and future milieu means a world that includes non-Indians). I have tried to show that tribalography comes from the native propensity for bringing things together, for making consensus, and for symbiotically connecting one thing to another. It is a cultural bias, if you will.

Choctaw/Cherokee author Louis Owens writes that the precedent for this wholeness is the oral tradition of American Indians:

> Just as significant is the fact that the concept of
> a single author for any given text, or of an individual
> who might conceive of herself or himself as the
> creative center and originating source of a story, or

of the individual autobiography, would have made as little sense to pre-Columbian Native Americans as the notion of selling real estate. For the traditional storyteller, each story originates and serves to define the people as a whole, the community. (Owens 1992: 9)

From the Glittering World by Navajo author Irvin Morris is one example of what I am calling tribalography. It is a collection of short stories that connect the Diné with their tribal history and contemporary lives. Throughout his book Morris makes no claims that the stories he tells belong to him alone. The book's subtitle, *A Navajo Story*, shows that he is not only telling stories that have been collected by his people, but the stories are about his journey through his people's experience. In essence, he is saying identity is determined by his history and the future.

The stories in the first section are the creation stories of the Diné that create dichotomies between man and woman, light and dark. Morris tells of a cosmic struggle for survival through flood and drought as well as the lineages of the original four clans of the Navajo. Following the introduction of Diné cosmology, Morris provides the reader with accounts of his family members. For example, Morris' great-grandmother witnesses the atrocities her people experienced when they were forced off their lands and marched into captivity. Therefore, Morris' stories transcend his own memories, but include those of his relatives and tribal community.

The modern stories in the final section are how Morris connects himself to the shiny and glittering world of the highways of the *bilagaanaa*, or white people. He juxtaposes this against the other world, the traditional *hooghan* life of his grandmother and great-grandmother. Often the telling is dismal. The average annual Diné per capita income for 1980 was only $2,400. Alcoholism takes young men from their homes on weeklong binges. But in the last story, titled "Meat and the Man," Morris offers a comedic version of Navajo life in the 90s.

An older white man and his dog called "Grabs-the-Meat" come to visit a Navajo family; they are uninvited guests. The *bilagaanaa*, a self-proclaimed tourist, speaks a little Navajo, badly. His car is broken down and he's hungry, so the family feeds him. Eventually he wants to hear stories so Grandma tells the man about Skinwalkers. The story is so powerful that he actually sees a Skinwalker outside the *hooghan* and faints with fright.

> "I told you not to tell those," said Jill, as they watched the man drive away the next morning. "I think you just about scared that man to death. What if he'd had a heart attack?"
>
> "He was awfully nosy," said Grandma.
>
> "But he talked Navajo," Jill's mother said.
>
> "Barely," corrected Grandma.
>
> "I'll bet he never forgets last night," said Jill.
>
> "Yup," said Jim. "He nearly shit his pants. You should have seen him."
>
> "*Yáadila*," said Jill.
>
> "I thought he was nice—and rather good-looking if you ask me," said Grandma. "What did you say his name was again?"
>
> (Morris 1997: 256-257)

The story ends with Grandma thinking she might take the old white man as a husband. By the end of Morris's tribalography, another possible future connection is made.

What is most significant about Morris' work is that while he is telling specific Navajo tribal history, culture, and his own revelatory stories, he also regards this textual space as a contemplative reflection of identity. What does it mean to be Navajo, but to connect with people who are not? The story continues.

Yanktonai author Susan Power's novel *The Grass Dancer* is another example of tribalography. Like Morris, Power has written a series of stories that are connected in a novel structure.

The story is set in North Dakota on the Standing Rock Sioux Reservation. Power steeps her readers in the connections between Dakota ancestors and the present-day culture. She tells Dakota stories through six central characters. Time travels counter-clockwise and there are multiple narrators giving their versions of events. This creates a multi-generational story that touches all the characters in the book. As each chapter unfolds, the reader is taken backwards in time until the final scenes of the book complete the beginning.

One of the central characters, Evie, a Dakota Sioux believes her father is a Blood Indian from Calgary. Her mother, Margaret Many Wounds, has told the story that she married Sonny Porter, and gave birth to twins, Evie and her sister Lydia. Evie has believed all her life that she inherited her father's looks, mannerisms, and temperament. Her creation story is that of the Dakota people. What we discover in Chapter Four, called "*MoonWalk*," is that Evie's father is Dr. Sei-ichi Sakuma, a Japanese surgeon from San Francisco. While it is important for Evie to know the identity of her father, she is not destroyed by the fact that he is Japanese because she has been raised with the Dakota, a people with powerful creation stories.

In a lecture at Grinnell College in 1999, Power talked about the stimulus that helped her create *The Grass Dancer* and her second novel, *War Bundles*. She said that she believes she is reclaiming American history in her novels of fiction.

> As a Native fiction writer I sometimes think of my work as consisting of little more than pointing out the bloody obvious. Ideas that Native peoples have been turning in their minds since the age of five can—once released into the mainstream discourse—find themselves plumped to the status of profundity. For this reason, I don't for a second claim to be covering new ground with my new novel, *War Bundles*, rather following trails familiar to a Native audience which sadly have proven to be revelatory to non-Natives exposed to early versions of the novel.

The message of *War Bundles* is incredibly simple. Native peoples, and their stories and histories are not a social studies unit of an interesting sub-category of American Literature to be haphazardly included in courses such as "Literatures of the Outsider in America," if at all. We are American history, we are American literature. Every track and trace of the American experience runs through our communities, our culture. We have been the transformers so much more than we are ever credited to have been. I am so tired of our image as the transformed—the lost, the dead, always those who are acted upon, always those who have been pushed to the edges, where we can be watched compassionately, nostalgically, seen as little more than a decorative fringe. I don't just want to learn how the writing of Louise Erdrich was influenced by William Faulkner, although that is a fascinating and necessary study, but additionally how so much of the material produced by white Southern writers and African-American writers reflects Native oral traditions. *War Bundles*, then, is not the development of a specifically "Native" history, but a reclamation of moments thought of as exclusively-peculiarly American. We (Natives) have participated in World Fairs and World Wars, witnessed the destruction of cities we also helped to raise; we were gangsters and outlaws, performers and writers. We were there. Always there. Still here. (Power 1999)

While these two books are models of what I call a tribalography, there are many others. Currently there are over two million American Indians in the United States, and most of these people, give or take a thousand, are writing stories. The first thing you may think is: LeAnne, you maniac, not every Indian in America is writing a book. I know it; some are making movies, or music videos for MTV.

Every Indian I meet is writing a story. A couple of summers ago while I was in Oklahoma conducting research and visiting family, I was invited to lecture at OK Choctaws, a non-polit-

ical organization in the Oklahoma City area. Many of the
elder members of OK Choctaws gathered every day for lunch
at the Salvation Army's Native American Center in downtown
Oklahoma City to share stories. After lecturing on some of the
historical documents I had found concerning Choctaws in the
early eighteenth century, I was asked to come back to help some
of the elders who wanted to tell their histories. What I found was
that all of the elders were writing stories that had been passed
down to them, stories of how their ancestors had survived the
1831 removal from Mississippi to Oklahoma. Our removal
began what is known as the Trail of Tears. The Choctaws I met
were incorporating the oral stories of their families with the
written documents of our removal. They were writing how their
ancestors had created new lives in nineteenth-century Indian
Territory, now called Oklahoma.

As we talked about their projects, their World War II
experiences, of growing up Choctaw, I realized that they
were doing what our ancestors had done for millennia: they
were pondering the mysteries of their experiences, telling
their stories, and creating a new discourse at the end of the
twentieth century. Whether they were speaking them into audio
tapes, writing them by hand, typing them into computers, or
recounting them to future generations of storytellers, Choctaws
were doing what Ojibwe author Gerald Vizenor describes as,
"...creat[ing] discourse with imagination" (Vizenor 1993: 187).
They were integrating oral traditions, histories, and experiences
into narratives and expanding our identity. Choctaws and other
American Indians are not only creating a future "literary past"
for American Indians, but a textual and literal past for non-
Indians, as well. If indeed our world "is what we say it is" (Tyler
1987: 171), as Tyler suggests, then a tribalography is a story that
links Indians and non-Indians in an expanding global covenant
chain. Uneasy tensions ensue. Of course. Not always happy,
most certainly, but inevitable for a good story.

In *Choctalking,* a collection of travel stories, I treat with animals, plants, peoples, spirits, ancestors, the mysteries of experiences residing in earthworks, and what little I know about matter in the universe. In "The Chaos of Angels," set in Louisiana with spirit turtles, a Haitian flight attendant, chickens and cats, the wily French colonizer of New Orleans, Jean-Baptiste Le Moyne de Bienville, (pronounced Zhan-Bap-teest Lay Moin day Bee-anh Veel, see Wikipedia) travels across time to make an appearance as a tree frog and later a bullfrog. In "Moccasins Don't Have High Heels," after a screaming match with a Houston bond trader and a client, I leave my job at a securities firm and go West just like the white settlers in the 1962 film *How the West Was Won* (but I don't kill anyone). Then at the Medicine Wheel near Lovell, Wyoming I receive some free advice from a red-tailed hawk that calls my name. (I know, it reads like one of those cheesy commercials for New Age shamans). Nevertheless, I return home and start working on my first novel, *Shell Shaker.*

Native stories have always been enormous in scope and in the telling of all creation, yet in a little over a century our stories have been pressed into the minuscule size of a grain of sand. A stereotype in feathers. So I hope to (re)complicate matters with international stories. "I Fuck Up in Japan" is the story of traveling to Okayama City during the 1993 United Nations International Year of the World's Indigenous People. I meet the Ainu, the indigenous people of Japan, and Burakumin people, the untouchables of Japan. It's no exaggeration to say that I made many cross-cultural mistakes and often made my hosts cry, along with myself and others I came into contact with. In "Carlos Castaneda lives in Romania" I become Humphrey Bogart and recite lines from the 1942 film *Casablanca* to Romanian border guards in order to cross into the city of Timişoara. Why I embody males, or on occasion multiple genders is because I believe that all matter, including human beings, can occupy multiple spaces at once. As Roxy Gordon suggests "everything touches everything, and everything is everything, and everything is very, very strange."

In the final story, "Embodied Tribalography" set in Oklahoma and Louisiana, I show how the animals and birds, and the land taught ancient Southeastern Natives how to play ball, live in the universe, and tell stories so powerful they create tribes.

I leave you with what my friend Craig Howe told me when I was a guest lecturer for a program called "Tribal Landscapes" at the Newberry Library in Chicago. I want you to repeat these words after me, because like my ancestors before me, I believe in the power of breath and mind. I am a *nukfoki*, teacher.

"Tribalism will not die, even if all the Indians do."

What I think Craig Howe is alluding to is that our stories are unending connections to past, present, and future. And, even if worse comes to the worst and our people forget where we left our stories, the birds will remember and bring them back to us.

Whe-ee, that's enough. I can tell you no more today!

Works Cited

Allen, Paula Gunn. *The Sacred Hoop: Recovering the Feminine in American Indian Tradition.* Boston: Beacon, 1986. Print.

Barreiro, José, ed. *Indian Roots of American Democracy.* Ithaca: Akwe:kon Press, Cornell University, 1992. Print.

Beauchamp, W.M. "The New Religion of the Iroquois." *The Journal of American Folk-Lore.* 10.38 (1897): 175-90. Print.

Bierhorst, John, ed. *Four Masterworks of American Indian Literature.* Tucson: University of Arizona Press, 1974 Print.

Bushnell, David I. "The Choctaw of Bayou Lacomb St. Tammany Parish Louisiana." Bureau of American Ethnology. Bulletin No. 48. Washington DC: Smithsonian Institution, 1909. Print.

Casablanca. Warner Brothers, 1942. Film.

Clayton, Nicola S. and Anthony Dickinson. "Episodic-like Memory during Cache Recovery by Scrub Jays." *Nature.* 395 (1998): 272-74. Print.

Clifford, James, and George Marcus, eds. *Writing Culture: The Poetics and Politics of Ethnography.* Berkeley: University of California Press, 1986. Print.

Cushman, H.B. *The History of the Choctaws, Chickasaws, and Natchez Indians.* Greenville, TX: Headlight Printing House, 1899. Print.

Fogelson, Raymond D. "The Ethnohistory of Events and Non-Events." *Ethnohistory.* 36.2 (1989): 133-47. Print.

Ford, Paul L., ed. *The Works of Thomas Jefferson.* 5. New York: Putnam, 1904-5. Print.

Grinde, Donald A. Jr. "Iroquoian Political Concept and the Genesis of American Government." José Barreiro, ed. *Indian Roots of American Democracy.* Ithaca: Akwe:kon Press, Cornell University, 1992. 47-66. Print.

How the West Was Won. Warner Brothers, 1962. Film.

Howe, LeAnne. "Danse D'Amour, Danse De Mort." Clifford E. Trafzer, ed. *Earth Sky, Song Spirit.* New York: Doubleday, 1993. 447-72. Print.

Lyons, Oren. "Land of the Free, Home of the Brave." José Barreiro, ed. *Indian Roots of American Democracy.* Ithaca: Akwe:kon Press, Cornell University, 1992. 30-35. Print.

---. "The Native Americans, Part 1: The Nations of the Northeast: The Strength and Wisdom of the Confederacies." TBS Productions, Inc. 1994. Interview.

Margulis, Lynn and Dorion Sagan. *Microcosmos Four Billions Years of Evolution from Our Microbial Ancestors.* New York: Summit Books, 1986. Print.

---. *What is Life?* New York: Simon & Schuster, 1995. Print.

Morris, Irvin. *From the Glittering World.* Norman: University of Oklahoma Press, 1996. Print.

Ortiz, Simon J. *Going for Rain.* New York: Harper, 1976. Print.

Owens, Louis. *Other Destinies: Understanding the American Indian Novel.* Norman: University of Oklahoma Press, 1992. Print.

Power, Susan. *Convocation.* Grinnell College Chapel, Iowa. Nov 1999. Formal lecture.

---. *The Grass Dancer.* New York: Putnam, 1993. Print.

Ruoff, A. LaVonne Brown. *American Indian Literatures: An Introduction, Bibliographic Review, and Selected Bibliography.* New York: The Modern

Language Association of America, 1990. Print.

Sarris, Greg. "The Native Americans, Part 2: The Tribal People of the Northwest: Living in Harmony with the Land." TBS Productions, Inc. 1994. Interview.

The Native Americans. TBS Productions, Inc., 1994. Film.

Tyler, Stephen A. *The Unspeakable: Discourse, Dialogue, and Rhetoric in the Postmodern World.* Madison: The University of Wisconsin Press, 1987. Print.

Venables, Robert W. "Choosing To Be Romans" José Barreiro, ed. *Indian Roots of American Democracy.* Ithaca: Akwe:kon Press, Cornell University, 1992. 67-106. Print.

Vizenor, Gerald, ed. *Narrative Chance: Postmodern Discourse on Native American Indian Literatures.* Norman: University of Oklahoma Press, 1993. Print.

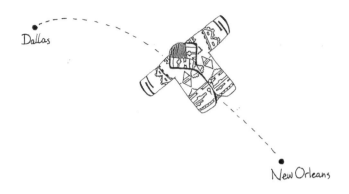

Dallas

New Orleans

When the Upper and Lower Worlds collide in the Between Worlds, there is a reaction in this World. Our ancestors called it Huksuba. Today we say chaos. Huksuba, or chaos, occurs when Indians and Non-Indians bang their heads together in search of cross-cultural understanding. The sound is often a dull thud, and the lesson leaves us all with a bad headache.

The Chaos of Angels

First there is the 2 A.M. heartbeat. The sound of my own breathing keeps me from sleep. I leave my bed for the comfort of the heated outdoor swimming pool and the relentless motion of water.

In New Orleans during the month of February delicate lukewarm rain falls. Fog exists. The night sky, neon and purple fire, compete for the senses.

In the central courtyard of the old world hotel, green french shutters hang on eighteenth-century windows. A gilded black woman peers down at me floating alone in the pool. I think I recognize her; we've crossed paths before and I know what comes next. I kick the water with my feet to begin a backstroke. Just then she opens the shuttered window and throws a red swatch of cloth tied with chicken feathers out the open window. The cloth flies away.

So this is how it's going to be. Another competition for the greatest suffering? Another contest on the pain of injustice? I continue floating in silence, pretending to ignore the tease. I'm busy. Intrigued only by the steaming water. Intimate with my own nakedness.

Again, there is a summons. A moment of red. A moment of deafness. And a crowless rooster flies from the arms of the black woman. She is craving attention. She will get it.

Onto the courtyard, with much ado, marched green-footed doormen with blue-tattooed mouths. Heartbeat for heartbeat, two-by-two, they are turtles in disguise.

Ancient ones out of the mud of the Mississippi River, they stand ready, watching over me. They've come to remind her that she's on Choctawan land, primordial, and indigenous, and that the conquering hordes only thought the Choctaw camps were abandoned, and the dogs were mute, and the stains on their hands, red colored and blue, were sweet scent.

"After all," I whisper aloud. "Have you ever seen what a turtle does to the reckless fowl who lands in its water space?"

Soon the black woman departs, laughing. "My turn," she says, disappearing into a soundless whirlwind.

The next day, I catch a flight out of New Orleans to Texas. I work for a securities firm headquartered in America's only true French city. My life in New Orleans, Monday through Friday, is temporary. As soon as our branch office is built I'll be relocated to "Big D," Dallas.

But I love New Orleans, though no one here seems to know it was once part of the greater Choctaw homelands stretching from Louisiana to Alabama. A pity. Our Choctaw Mother Mound is in Mississippi. The beginning of our existence as a people begins at our mound, Nanih Waiya, our birthplace. Perhaps it is our own fault. My Choctaw ancestors helped Jean-Baptiste Le Moyne, Sieur de Bienville establish the first French colony at the mouth of the Mississippi via our trading networks with other tribes.

I often haunt the city's oldest establishments in search of the spirit of Jean-Baptiste Le Moyne, Sieur de Bienville. That may sound a little whacked, but I'm certain the bastard is still hanging around dead drunk. Everyone I know here is drunk fifty-percent of the time. People in New Orleans say, "likkah" for liquor, Absolut for vodka. I myself am drunk fifty-percent of the time, especially since becoming a regular at the Napoleon House, a two-hundred-year-old bar with an intense, often morose atmosphere (although I admit I'm often there in the wee hours before dawn).

On the plane back to Dallas, a mysterious flight attendant offers me a strong red drink. Red again. Her Haitian accent is lilting and I think she's beautiful. She cups her hands around my hands when she gives me the red drink. I swallow it without breathing, something I learned at the Old Absinthe House on the corner of Rue Bienville in the French Quarter, my second favorite rendezvous with destiny. Egad, there's that name again, "Bienville." His history from 1701-1743 is wholly intertwined with the Choctaws and there's no reason to think that knotted mass has been untangled.

I suddenly realize that I've been Mickey Finned and am about to pass out. I think about the smoothness of the Haitian woman's hands as my mind goes woozy. Her long, slender fingers remind me of the old adage, "Jean-Baptiste Le Moyne, Sieur de Bienville, his hands helped shape the New World." *Damn, I vowed not to let this happen again, I'm the narrator in a movie about a French frog.*

THE VOICE-OVER

Bienville still roams the streets of New Orleans, the city he platted out of swampland in 1718. Ears back, eyes rolling in his head, he more resembled a tree frog hugging a lamppost than a jazzman fingering a saxophone. But the shape shifter was him.

My Choctaw ancestors called Bienville, *Filanchi*, which is short for "Our Frenchman, the Nail Biter." They liked him, although he was nervous and could never take a joke. The first time they invited him for dinner, he started making problems that have continued until now.

Back in the old days, dining with the tribe was not at all like having dinner with your next-door neighbor. No, Choctaw dinners were meant to be experienced. These weeklong, elaborately arranged soirees were evenings of collective communication. Dinner guests were always selected carefully, juxtaposing good jokers with good listeners. Visitors were also expected to report in great detail about other tribal groups, gossip being one of our favorite sports. However, what Bienville did before the meal began was to toss some third-rate glass beads on the ground and ask if my relatives would trade them for "*un morceau de terre*" (a morsel of land).

This glitch in decorum put a damper on the cross-cultural understanding between the French and Choctaw peoples. Such was this breach of etiquette that my relatives decided to have some fun with him.

"You want us to exchange land for these flimsy discount beads? What kind of chicanery are you trying to pull on *vos amis les sauvages*?" (Your friends the savages?)

"*Ne vendez pas le peau de l'ours avant de l'avoir tuee.*" (Do not sell the bearskin before you've killed the bear.) "*N'est-ce pas, mon ami?*" My grandmother loved to mock his speech.

"Besides," she continued, "the English traders are giving us some terrific deals on black powder muskets." (You may or may not remember that the rivalry between the French and the English traders was at a fever pitch in the early eighteenth century.)

At this point Bienville's expression underwent a complete and violent change. He started in on my relatives and would not let up.

"When zee English and your friends, zee Chickasaws, were beating zee shish kebob out of you in 1702, who came in with zee foreign policy muscle to save your corn, your potatoes, your tomatoes, your pumpkins, your beans, and your yellow-squashed asses? Just who?" shouted the little Frenchman with confidence.

Bienville pointed to my relatives seated before him and he continued. "Just who used zeir swag to provide you with weapons and gun powder, interest free? Tell me? Any one of you who thinks it was zee English, raise your hands!

"Ah-ha, no takers! *Bon.* We are getting somewhere. Just who…"

My grandmother near went deaf from listening to this tirade. Before *Filanchi* could tune-up for another crybaby episode, she called together a special session of all the men and women to decide what to do with him. Some wanted to kill him right on the spot, others thought of torture. Elder heads prevailed. They traded him the swampland that belonged to our cousins, the Bayougoulas. That's right. Swampland.

In return, my relatives received some first rate axes, some metal pots, and a dozen used musket rifles. They also took the flimsy glass beads off his hands. When my relatives told the Bayougoulas what happened, they all went four-paws-up laughing because the land that had been traded was a huge floodplain. Six months out of every year it was knee deep in water, snakes, and alligators. Nowhere were there more mosquitoes than on that piece of land. Most days of the year the air was so thick with mosquitoes that you couldn't distinguish one person from another ten paces a way.

Naturally my relatives shared the trade goods with the Bayougoulas and the whole wheedling affair was largely forgotten by both peoples. Then one afternoon a group of Choctaws were tramping through the area and stumbled across *Filanchi* and his soldiers, now get this, camping in two feet of water. Imagine their surprise. My grandfather called to him from higher ground. (Grandfather was not an imbecile, after all.)

"*Filanchi*, what are you doing down there?"

Well—Bienville started in on Grandfather just as he had with my grandmother. He was flailing his hands like a lunatic and babbling on and on. The gist of his harangue, and I hope I'm not misquoting him, was that the land was his. The end.

"Messieurs Chahtas, as you remember, I have traded for zeese land fair and square, and by our Holy Reverend Father, I will defend it to zee death."

Filanchi then went on to say that the bayous had overflowed so furiously that he and his men had been four months in waist high water. My grandfather had to turn away to keep from laughing himself silly.

Filanchi then staggered. "Your femmes assured me zat zeese place was never inundated. Look at zeese mess! I do not understand? Zeese is all your fault."

Poor thing. He could barely see to curse my grandfather because the mosquitoes had stung him in both eyes, and he had tried to cover his swollen face with a sort of bandage-like thing. It was in this sad moment that we realized the truth of the matter. Our Frenchman, The Nail Biter, did not have all his oars in the water. Since advice is the most repulsive of all faults, showing disrespect for the feathers of common sense in others, my relatives left him there soaked to the skin, standing in the middle of "New France." And it wasn't until much later that we realized the joke was on us.

Now, as I have said into eternity, there was a continual rhythm of give and take among Indian tribes in the Southeast. We gave, they gave. That's how things had been done for about 2,000 years, until *Filanchi* showed up. I'm not kidding; no one had ever wanted land. Forever. His desire was an anomaly. This changed all rules of government-to-government cooperation. We had no idea how to proceed.

Oh, I take that back. My relatives had come across this kind of thing before. Grandmother loved to tell the story about some foreign tribe—I think they were from Spain or Portugal—anyway, they ventured into our territory and just demanded all the tribe's gold. Choctaws never had gold. Not really. Occasionally they could trade for it down South, but my relatives never found gold to be particularly useful. However, these spiritual shoppers would not take "no" for an answer. First they begged, pestered, then threatened:

"*O nos dais el maldito oro, o os cortamos el cuello!*"

Finally our men gave in. They heated up what little gold they had into a fiery red liquid and poured it down the tourists' throats.

As I finish telling Grandmother's story, I lose my concentration again. My wooziness tricks me into thinking I'm back at my writing desk, working on another chapter of my novel, or filming a scene of an avant-garde video I want to produce. But my mind is in chaos. Suddenly, Bienville steps into my brain with his saxophone hooked on his neck chain. He begins playing a little melody, but he stops long enough to deliver his own breathy narration into an invisible microphone.

"It is early morning, fog crawls along the street in the French Quarter. A single young woman is window-shopping. In zee background zeir are other stores, other shops, but zey are out of focus. Zeir are other people milling around, but zey are in zee background and blurry. Out of focus.

"*La femme* stops in front of a large storefront window. She wears a white raincoat and carries a white plastic umbrella.

"Our heroine stares into zee bedroom shop window. She sees two intertwined, faceless figures lying on zee bed. Zee figures are covered completely by white cotton sheets and beneath zee sheets zey are wearing white full-body stockings. Zee white rain woman believes zey are two murdered corpses, until zey begin coupling as if by an automated timer."

Beinville plays another riff on his saxophone, then continues his soliloquy:

"Zee stocking people begin to make love. One tenderly mounts zee other. Slowly zey hunch in heartbeat rhythm. Zee lover's faces and hair color remain unseen to our heroine, her breathing quickens and she wets her lips with her tongue and chants in sync with zee rhythmic lovers, fuck me. Fuck me!"

"Oh God, zees is good!" says Bienville.

"*Help!*" I sit straight up in my seat. I look around to see if anyone hears me. Obviously the red drink was a strong concoction, a potion cooked up by my nemesis, the flight attendant from Haiti. Just as I believe I'm coming to my senses, someone shakes me awake.

IT looks like a bug-eyed man, with thick wide lips, wearing cowboy clothes and an obnoxious leather belt with the capital letters B-U-L-L etched across the silver buckle.

"Are you practicing safe sex, gal? Holy Cow. Look out the window. The earth is much bigger than I imagined. Wait until Grandmother hears about this."

I slap myself in the face, but IT is still seated next to me.

"Do I know you?" I ask. "And what do you mean…am I practicing safe sex?"

"Of course you know me. But I don't know what I mean. Not anymore. Thoughts just pop in my head. I guess it's because you were thinking about sex and water, and power. I just say what pops in my head."

"Rivvit, rivvit…Oops."

The thing cups a slender hand over its mouth and looks at me frog-eyed. Then IT chatters on like I'm an old friend, not really speaking a language, just mimicking a language. Every few phrases are in English, but they're gibberish.

"You know," it says, "I think cats and alligators are related. They have those same funny eyes. Slanted pupils. And, you know alligators and birds are related. Hollow bones. I think cats could fly once upon a time. You know how they're always climbing trees and they don't mind when you throw them off buildings. Wow! Look down there. Is that a lake? Rivvit, rivvit... *Uh-hem*, excuse me."

I am alive. I'm flying in a jet somewhere between Louisiana and Texas. However, judging from this thing's obsession with cats, I realize I'm staring at an ancient French frog. A holdover from last night's spirit world rivalry.

You see, cats held great mystery to eighteenth-century French people. Cats appealed to poets like Baudelaire, and yet to the citizens of Aix-en-Provence, cats were used like baseballs before cheering crowds as they smacked kitten and tomcat alike into the nearest wall. But that's not the worst of it. They also ate cat brains when they wanted to be invisible, provided the gray matter was still hot.

The French also made a mixed drink from cat feces and red wine that they called a tonic for colic. (And they called Indians, *les sauvages*.)

It was the French who coined the phrase, "Patient as a cat whose paws are being grilled." They also believed that cats were witches in disguise, so brave Frenchmen and Frenchwomen devised remedies to save themselves from danger by maiming "Kitty-kitty."

They cut kitty's tails, clipped kitty's ears, smash kitty's legs, tore or burned kitty's fur, and hanged kitty—until almost dead. The thinking in France, at the time, was that a mutilated housecat would be too embarrassed to walk into a church and cast a spell. Go figure.

The cat was also symbolic of "Old World" sexual culture: *Le chat, la chatte, le minet,* roughly translates into the English expression for "pussy." If a Frenchman petted a kitten, he would have success in courting a mate. If a Frenchwoman stepped on a cat's tail she would not get her man.

Cats were strictly Old World. So were barnyard chickens. Both were foreign imports to the New World. I am proud to say that American Indians never ate cats. We preferred deer, bear, buffalo, corn, beans, squash, pumpkins, potatoes, onions, tomatoes, chocolate, pecans, and of course wild turkey, a native to the forests of the Western Hemisphere. As far as the Choctaws were concerned, chickens were entirely too small to satisfy serious Choctaw diners.

After looking more closely at the French frog seated next to me, I recognized "IT" for who it was. Bienville, that big phony, was disguised as a bullfrog. I glance around the cabin for the Haitian woman, knowing she must be in on this latest cross-cultural joke, but she is nowhere to be found.

Then all at once he starts in on me just as he had with Grandmother: "You know I like flying," he says coyly. "Of course, this can't compare to riding in a red 1963 Ford Galaxy convertible with the top down listening to Nancy Sinatra sing *These Boots Are Made For Walking.* Then he babbles on in an almost random stream of consciousness.

"I love my cowboy boots. Whaddaya think of 'em? I sing myself electronic! You know why Sitting Bull was a star? It was because he had good P.R. Reality is a rubber band you can pull in any direction."

I clinch my fists and scream. "Shut up, shut up, shut up! I want you to shut up and go away. Who sent you?"

A blonde flight attendant walks past us, and we both smile at her as if nothing is wrong. He looks away, rueful and uneasy. He nervously bites a loose fingernail. Finally, he pulls his wide lips together until his mouth resembles an egg. "You should have remembered that for every action there is a reaction. I don't know how much that vulgar display of enchanted alchemy cost you last night while you were, *ah-hem,* swimming. But I think you lost Grandmother's respect. She always says you always act like 'Puss 'n Boots'."

"My grandmother told you no such thing. If you don't stop lying I'm going to put you in a mayonnaise jar and screw the lid on tight."

My threat has little impact. The banter stops when he pulls a tiny saxophone from underneath his seat and begins playing "Beautiful Dreamer" by Stephen Foster. I close my eyes and try to dream him back to the Old Absinthe House. But I fail and slip into another chaotic vision.

The images that come back to me are so far removed by generations that the pain they carry is slight. They roll forward like silent videos of something that happened, not to me, not to my bones that embody these memories, but to the part of me they are.

My first memories are of complete darkness. You would not call them memories, but something given by blood from her, while she still carried me in her body.

First, there is the sound of water and heartbeat.
A call from the Upper World to the Lower World.
Chahtas crawled up through the mud of the Nanih Waiya, and into the sun's light. We washed ourselves off and combed our long hairs.

Some of us lived like crayfish.
Some of us lived like turtles.
Some of us lived like coiled snakes, end to end.
Some of us lived like people.

We danced, prayed, practiced our songs, learned to hunt, and grew the tall green corn that balanced our lives for 2000 years before the whites forcibly removed us to Oklahoma. After the long walk on the trail of bad memories to Indian Territory, our past experiences seemed to change us.

I can see my relatives now walking west at sunset. Fireballs are bursting around their heads. Then my grandmother falls down. Something is wrong.

"Get up, Grandmother, get up." I pull at her shoulders but she doesn't move. "Somebody help!"

Suddenly, I run to find help, but I'm lost in a tangle of trees. Lost without my family. In the next moment, someone shakes me awake, again. The French frog has disappeared, but the woman from the hotel courtyard sits next to me.

"You called?" she asked. "Haven't you forgotten that the French took some of your Choctaw ancestors to Haiti? They made a new home and children in that new place. You seemed to forget last night that we are sisters. Not competitors. Maybe the joke is on you, after all?

I wince remembering my hubris. "Are you finished with me?" I ask, trying to hide my embarrassment.

"Not ever," she answers. "Come with me."

I follow her to the first class section of the plane. Sitting in the front row is Grandmother watching *Star Wars* on the big screen. When she turns to look at me, her warm smile pulls me into the empty seat next to her.

"I love this movie, don't you?" she whispers. "Darth Vader wears such wonderful headgear."

"Grandmother, what are you doing here?" I ask.

"First, she played a joke," she says to my sister who has taken the aisle seat across from her. "Then you forgot your sense of humor, and tried to shame her. So I finished the joke. We all must work hand in hand; that is the lesson. And now it's time for Jean-Baptiste to return to his group. Enough's enough." She turns back to the movie.

"*Shu-u-sh-h*, this is where they blow the Death Star to pieces," she says.

I look at her with wonder. "Grandmother, I don't know how to feel about what has happened."

She whispers. "Never forget we are all alive! All people, all animals, all living things; and what you do here affects all of us everywhere. What we do affects you, too."

She pats my face and begins talking in a normal voice. "Our ancestors survived wars, the Europeans, diseases, and removal from our homelands. Now, my group, which is many generations older than your group, is learning how to survive the chaos of all these angels. It's what we've started to call "a cross-cultural afterlife, living challenge."

She smiles and says, "It beats banging our heads together."

With that, she grabs my sister's hand and my hand, and the three of us watch Darth Vader zooming alone across the universe in a tiny spaceship. In the tribal ethos, being isolated from one's relatives is the worst horror we can imagine, so we hold each other tight and wonder what will happen next.

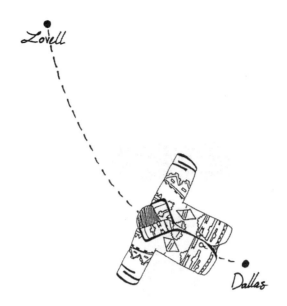

Lovell

Dallas

Moccasins Don't Have
High Heels

Go West young man, go West. The words reverberate like an echo in my head as I sit on a rocky ledge watching a red-tail hawk circle the perimeter of the Medicine Wheel in the Big Horn Mountains near Lovell, Wyoming. A windswept plateau plays host to the spectacular eighty-foot-wide-wheel made of enormous rocks with twenty-eight spokes extending from the rim to the center. Together plateau and wheel spin in the glorious winds of summer. An illusion, I know, because the Medicine Wheel is a place American Indians come for vision quests and healing ceremonies.

"*Go West,*" the giant hawk seems to say as it wings by me. Eye level. It's the damnedest thing, he flies at eye level, and then soars up, then down. And even in the falling, he breaks and runs again for the sun. I'm certain this bird is not real. Ceremonies live here. I stretch out on the ledge like a lizard and watch how the bright sun garments the ponderosa pines below. No sound or noise of any kind. No complaints either.

The year is 1989 and I marvel at how clean the air smells at an elevation of 9,565 feet. Although I'm not the man Horace Greeley imagined when he wrote, *Go West young man, go West*, (after all I'm a Choctaw woman), I've been rescued by my friend from Texas, Cara Waggoner, a landscape artist who wants to paint her way westward to the Rockies. She drives us north and west out of Texas. We stay in Colorado a few days before heading into Wyoming. We crisscross the state over a two-week period and linger in Cheyenne and Laramie. The fresh air, new environment and the unfamiliar terrain are supposed to help me escape the securities industry and memories of day trades that linger like a living body inside me.

"Ed Hardy," I say, "Need a bid. 10 million treasuries due Nov 98 at 8¾."

"Hold, I'm on with New York. 98 to the buck, Darlin'."

I go back to the client with 97, 30/32, as if we're trading mortgage-backs, shaving off two for the commission. It's been a normal day in our Dallas office. Everyone on our Houston trading desk has been spitting up blood, eating, or talking to his or her trading buddies on Wall Street. Occasionally, I overhear on the speakerphone one of the traders lying to his wife about his plans after work. Now our client, an official from a state agency, says she wants to blow out of ten million treasuries.

I tell her, "hold." Everyone is still cordial. Polite. No cursing. Wall Street traders and sales people are notorious for purpling the air with expletives.

I cut back to Houston. "Okay, Edward, I'll sell you 10 million 8¾, Nov of 98, at 98."

"Hold on, Darlin'," he says, "97, 28. The market's moving."

I check back with her. She's screaming and gnashing her teeth. A nanosecond and she's down $12,500, but she still wants to do it.

"I'll sell 10 million Nov 8¾ at 97, 28."

"It's falling, Darlin'," Ed's voice drolls, "97, 26."

I go back with. "97, 24."

A loud scream tears through my headset; she's down another two. Suddenly I'm a motherfucker. I sweat cannonballs, but remain calm. More screaming into my ear and I can just barely make out this low roar, "Yes. Get me out!"

I holler, "What's happening, Edward?"

He comes back with, "97, 22."

"Do it."

He counters, "97, 18."

"Do it. Do it. Do it!"

He confirms, "You're done Darlin', 97 and a half."

I go earsplitting crazy, "What the fuck! Ed, are you working for the Japanese now?" Ed clicks off.

I go back to our customer, remember to smile into the headset, "Hello, Ma'am. You're done at 97, 14." Eighteen seconds and she just lost $56,250. (Not that much really.) More shrieking at higher octaves until I'm sure only a cat can hear what she's saying. Then she's back to cursing me, says she sending an Iranian terrorist to our office. She tells me she'll never do business with our firm again. She says she's putting a curse on all the unborn children in our firm. She threatens to catch the next plane to Dallas and come into town and rip off my tits. (Not again.)

"Yes. I am so-o-o sorry. The market was falling and we were the best bidder on the street. My trader says there's a rumor the Japanese are going to...

(I cannot type what she says.)

"No way did I get to you, Ma'am. There's no way I'd do that. I am telling the truth. Really. I'll call your assistant with figures. Don't worry about a thing. I'll take care of you. Listen, let me send you some theatre tickets for a New York show. We've been meaning to send you tickets to your favorite Broadway musical. Sure. Anytime. I'll even meet you in New York and take you out to dinner. I was just there recently and it was a real throw-down. Wherever you say. Don't worry about a thing. After all, it's not *our* money.

Click.

"Hello?" I wait about three beats before jerking off my headset. "Ah, fuck it, I quit."

Actually I didn't quit. I always said I was quitting every day of the week for four and a half years, but to tell you the truth, I loved it. I loved working on the bond side of the financial markets. But after the crash of the bond market in 1987, many client portfolios were underwater, worth much less than they paid for the treasuries, mortgage-backs, or other financial instruments. Our office limped along for another year and half until our home office in New Orleans eventually consolidated the bond departments. On a cold February morning we shut down the Dallas operation and left one by one. I was the last one to leave, but took my time... a final look around.

Lying around the office were things my bond buddies had left behind. There was a gold golf putter, a gray donut cushion from a co-worker's hemorrhoid operation, a couple of plastic handguns, an orange Nerf ball that had traveled with us from Dallas to New Orleans, and back again to Big D. One of the guys had given me a political button that said, "If God So Loved America, why did he create Democrats?" (I was the only Dem in an entire industry of Repubs.)

I looked out across an incredible view of the Dallas skyline again, picked up one of the toy handguns I bought at a children's store and brought into the office. I struck a pose just like Inspector Harry Callahan, (Clint Eastwood, also a Republican) and shot at the speakerphone on my desk. It had once been our lifeline to the trading desk in Houston and I wanted to kill it for all the times it had failed our group, failed everyone. But unlike Dirty Harry in the movies, I was only holding a toy .44 Remington Magnum.

So as a gesture of the passage of time and the memories of the financial conquests our unit had made and lost over the past four years, I symbolically put the gold putter in my boss's chair, gave the chair a spin, (counterclockwise, of course) a metaphor for turning back time, and watched it silently go-around-and-around. Eventually the chair stood still, and I walked out the door, alone.

I have nightmares. Each night I dream I'm back in the bond business, only this time my friends and I sit in grade school desks, all in a row. We're working for, like, this drive-in bank in a shopping center. In my dreams our bond trader is in the same room with us watching *I Love Lucy*. I'm working for minimum wage and selling Indian beads, real estate, and, of all things, ice cream to passersby who wander in off the street asking if they can buy a billion dollars of mortgage-backed securities.

Suddenly a bomb explodes in the trading room. The glass case that holds the Indian beads blows apart. Glass and trade beads blow across the wilderness. I don't know why the wilderness always shows up in my dreams like some kind of freaky Frederic Remington wilderness painting, but it does. In my dreams the ice cream always turns to water. We pull a white sheet over the body of our bond trader. Poor Ed Hardy, he's underwater. We know he's dead. Lady Luck has left us forever. Man, she got to us.

At the Medicine Wheel, I turn on my side, lost, but for the memories I bring. The rock ledge forces me to sit up and stretch my back. The joy of July winds caresses my face and I search the site for Cara, who has set up her easel near one of the cairns and is beginning to paint. I wave and she finally sees me. Cara raises her brush high in the air and returns to her work. Above me the hawk kettles and calls. Beyond, a dark brood of pines whine to the land that gathers more stones around the wheel. This is not superstition.

"What else do you miss? Say everything," says the wind.

I shout. "When I left, I wasn't leaving my job I was leaving my bond family. Probably for good. I threw away my high heels and put on moccasins. Everything was getting to me." Looking skyward for the bird I say in a normal voice, "You may want to know why I stayed with it? Why I did it? —

"The Money! The Moola, Benjamins, bread, clams, coin, lettuce, smackers. Crap! The money got to me."

I look around at the landscape, and the Medicine Wheel. I'm talking to myself, the wind, and a bird. I'm afraid of these visions.

We'd arranged the trip to the Medicine Wheel to be the final leg of our westward journey. From Lovell, we would drive south through Colorado and make our way back to Texas. So before the Medicine Wheel, we visited Fort Laramie and sang *America the Beautiful* and discovered that Wyoming lands are lousy with antelope. Their white tails glisten in the sun. They're easy to see but are hard to kill, unless, say, you're in a Ford Bronco driving forty miles an hour down a mountain road. *Ah-hem.*

For the most part there are no cars in Wyoming, only pickups and a few houses spread out over the state. No nuclear power plants, either. It's an isolationist's dream. Maybe it's a developer's dream. When asked about clear-cutting our national forests, former President Reagan once quipped, "Well, once you've seen one redwood, you've seen 'em all." Reagan has been a role model for developers all across America. So I figure maybe Disneyland will someday develop Wyoming into a kind of a Frederic Remington theme park. The Old West like it never was. At one time there were Arapaho, Cheyenne, Crow, Shoshoni, and Ute living in Wyoming. One of the tribes, the Cheyenne, was removed to Oklahoma, and the group that stayed was renamed Southern Cheyenne.

Eventually Cara and I made our way to Jackson Hole, Wyoming. It was Old West Days and Alta, a friend of Cara's from Dallas, had flown in for the party.

When a band of Shoshoni begin dancing a round dance and playing the drum and asking everyone to join in for friendship, Alta got nervous. She said I scalped her in a previous life, and the tom-toms get to her. (No, I'm not kidding.)

"LeAnne, what are those drums saying? Does it make you

want to go to war? Is that drumbeat getting to you the way it's getting to me? How does it make you feel?"

Alta was near hysterical by this time. I thought I'd help her along.

"Yeah, it's getting to me, Alta. And you're getting to me. Again. Maybe you should go inside before I reach for my knife and *yatahey*; you know what happened last time."

Alta seemed struck dumb. Cara finally dragged Alta away by coaxing her into a bead shop. Alta looked back to see if I was serious, but knowing Alta (and I don't), I think what she really wanted was for me to make medicine with her. Trade her some land for beads. Make amends in this life for what she believed I'd done to her in a past life. Not ten minutes before that bizarre outburst, Alta had said that crystals talk to her. Tell her what to do. Tell her who she's been in a previous life. And where she's going in the next life, and what's getting to her, and what's getting to me. But like who am I to quibble with spiritualists? Some of the most successful religious folk out West (Mormons) say God lives on planet Kolob. *I know, I know*, he doesn't actually live there he just broadcasts from a planet close to Kolob. Besides, I talk to the wind and birds.

Actually, when you're an American Indian, you learn spiritualists and other religious folk are always telling you how Indians feel about everything.

"Don't you Indians, like *ah-h*, like *ah-h*, see yourselves as just transcending this time–space continuum thing? Yeah, like you all practiced this kind of Indian-Zen thing? Right?"

While I was in Jackson Hole, I met Priscilla Davis, this really nice white teacher. She told me that she had taught on the Pine Ridge Reservation. She said that Indians don't talk much, but that when we say something it's always profound and fraught with meaning.

I just looked at her.

"Oh yeah," she said, "and Indian women are very jealous of their men."

I deadpanned. "White woman speak truth!"

Shortly before the trip out west with Cara, I attended an archaeological conference in South Dakota on the Ethical Treatment of the Dead and Indians. I listened to dozens of archaeologists tell us how we felt about the time–space continuum thing. About what diseases killed us the fastest. Smallpox, measles, scarlet fever, rheumatic fever, tuberculosis, whooping cough, chickenpox, and diphtheria are all diseases brought to us by the Columbus Exchange Program. Come to think of it, I've had the measles, scarlet fever, rheumatic fever, and chickenpox, and I've died several times. Who do I sue for damages?

One man, a physical anthropologist, lectured on how back in the old days, one hundred years ago, Indians had small gene pools. He theorized that we must have practiced incest. But by grinding our skeletons and sawing our skulls apart for analysis he hadn't found any evidence of incest. Mr. Hyde, aka Dr. Jekyll, said he had spent his entire academic career dissolving our skeletal remains, and that while the facts were inconclusive, he was going to keep on looking. Keep on cutting. Keep on trying. Keep on digging us up. He was finally going to get to the truth, somehow.

In 1971, an Iowa road crew unearthed a cemetery. Twenty-six of the bodies were white. They also found one Indian woman and her baby. The whites were placed in new coffins and reburied. The Indian and her baby were boxed up and sent to Iowa City for study.

They got to her, all right. Does that get you, too?

It seems it wasn't enough that the aliens wanted to capture our souls for their god, they wanted to own our physical bodies, too. That's why in 1989 Governor Bill Clements of Texas vetoed a bill that would have protected unmarked Indian graves in the

Lone Star State. The collectors and grave robbers from Dallas can still get to Indian graves in Texas without being charged with a crime. Ironically, Governor Clements told an audience at a state archaeologist meeting in 1989 that his fantasy profession was to be an archaeologist. But he went into politics instead.

Governor Bill got to us, all right.

Edward Galeano summed it up perfectly when he said, "Throughout America, from north to south, the dominant culture acknowledges Indians as objects of study, but denies them as subjects of history. Indians have folklore, not culture, they practice superstitions, not religion, they speak dialects, not languages, they make crafts, not arts..."

Yet, if I had to say only one thing American Indians represented in America's history it would be land. We had the land, the colonizers wanted land, and killed for it. We didn't know about selling it, or trading it in a winner-take-all market. In 1692 Dutch settlers built the Wall path to keep out the Indians. The Wall path joined the banks of the east river with those of the Hudson River on the west. Wall path was later named Wall Street and apparently by the 1980s, I was the only American Indian that had crept over the wall and into the business of buying and selling the air, water, land, people, words.

"Wanna bid? Maybe to trade Japan for China? Just warning you: you're going to have to sell short. However it works, it won't be a pretty picture."

I stand up and shake off the visions of buying and selling the air, the water, and even myself. It wasn't my intent to bring those memories into being here, but I couldn't help it, I carry them inside me. What to do? The red-tailed hawk returns on an updraft of wind. He screams three times as he flies around the Medicine Wheel and then back toward me. Within an instant my hands glow bright red as if they've been burned, and I hear the hawk whiz right by my head. I walk quickly to where Cara is painting and show her my hands. She looks concerned, and briefly I wonder if my entire body is on fire.

"Crazy as it sounds, the hawk said my name. Look what happened to my hands."

"Maybe you're having a stroke?" she says.

"Cara."

"Just kidding. What does it mean?"

"I think I'm supposed to write the stories I carry inside me."

She looks into my being as a painter might see a landscape whose aim is not conveying reality, but the autonomy of space. She does not drop her gaze. I feel exposed. Eventually we turn back to the Medicine Wheel locked in the moment, and listen.

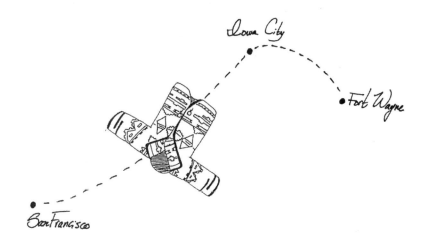

Iowa City

Fort Wayne

San Francisco

How I Lost Ten Pounds

Strange things happen when you're an unknown Choctaw author on a US book tour. Sure some people say stupid things like:

"I thought all the Chock Toes were dead."

"I didn't know Chak-tows had a language."

"So if the tribes are different—why do all you Indians have the same name?"

While hearing such remarks is somewhat painful, there's no limit to the amount of fun you can have with the people who make them. They become part of the extraordinary events you will want to scribble down and savor.

Dear Diary,

> *Today the judge said that with good behavior I can be released in...*

Just kidding. However, in the final ten days of my "first book tour," I lost ten pounds. I should probably say that Choctaw people consider a little paunch a sign of wellbeing. In fact, the old timers in our community used to greet one another by saying *"Chi niah katimi?"* How's your fat? Though today American starlets and pop idols are as skinny as refugees, my tribe considers a little heft a good thing. Therefore I was more than a little concerned about my quick weight loss.

An examination of self-help books at the Barnes and Noble proved *no* help, although I did find *Trichotillomania and You* a fascinating read. Obsessive hair pulling wasn't the problem, loss of body fat was.

As I think back on the book tour adventure, I believe my appetite began to wane shortly after a particularly discouraging reading in Ft. Wayne, Indiana. The event was an anomaly when compared with the rest of the stops on the book tour. Not only had the audience actually heard of Native Americans, they were still fighting the war of 1791 between Little Turtle and the American general Arthur St. Clair. FYI, most historians agree that this battle was "America's Waterloo." Over 700 of St. Clair's men were killed—compared with only 40 Miami—thereby leaving the United States Army with a sum total of just over 300 men.

"Were your people, the Choctaw, aware of the war that the Miami were waging against us, the poorest settlers in the colonies?" asked an elderly woman in the audience.

"I'm sure they were," I replied.

"What did they think?"

"Well, I didn't mean to imply that there are documents that show the Choctaw knew of the event and commented on it," I said. "Rather, there are stories of…"

"Little Lady, I'm asking about Little Turtle's war."

"Yes, I know, and…"

She cut me off again. "Did your tribe ally against the settlers? And if so, do you know why the Indians would assault us in this way?" She raised an eyebrow and scrutinized me.

I tried to scrutinize back. She looked to be in her early 80s. A handsome woman, she was nicely dressed in a bright periwinkle shift with matching earrings. I felt kindly towards her, even though she'd admitted she was a descendent of General St. Clair.

"Speak up."

"Um, no ma'am, but I have an idea this was over land issues and sovereignty over Native lands. These are complicated events in tribal histories—and besides, at the time the Choctaw had our own issues to deal with in Mississippi nearly seven hundred miles away."

"So the Choctaw stayed on the sidelines, huh," said the descendant of St. Clair.

I wasn't sure why the old woman was so hostile to me and my tribe, but I had been taught as a child to never fight with elders in public, especially those who are white, rude, and offensive.

"The Choctaw are a people who try to deliberate on all sides so we can make prudent decisions on how to avoid harm whenever possible. We practice caring for all living things, animate and inanimate. Choctaw people are the essence of due diligence. In my book I explain how we have always made good relationships with newcomers. Failure to do so would be considered neglect."

She looked at me for a moment, and then stood up, regal like the Queen of England.

"Quisling."

She actually said that with a straight face. Then she turned to leave, followed by her consort and a dozen of her entourage marching single file out of the bookstore.

It wasn't until I arrived at Prairie Lights Bookstore in Iowa City that I began to feel a connection with readers again. Iowa City is a book town and knowledgeable people turn out for readings. I was not disappointed. A local woman brought a Choctaw dog to my reading. Evidently she'd heard that a Choctaw author was coming to town and decided to bring the dog and introduce us. (I swear I'm telling the truth.)

"The dog is a Catahoula, which roughly means 'lake' in Choctaw," she says.

I smiled and nodded like a bobblehead glued to the dashboard of a car. I had no idea what the hell she was talking about. But after the reading she told me to call her "Edith," because we were going to be lifelong friends.

She rubbed her dog's head. "You know in the Atchafalaya Basin, he can climb trees."

Oh my. I looked at the woman, who was smiling like the Cheshire cat. I wanted to say, *Of course the dog can climb trees, he's trying to get away from alligators,* but thought better of it.

"He comes from a long line of Choctaw ancestors in Mississippi, just like you," she said.

The woman with the dog was starting to piss me off. As she and her damn dog followed me outside, I decided to look for the nearest bar.

"He's a seizure dog," she said, suddenly. I turned to inspect the poor creature. I tried to hide my sorrow. He was wearing a white medical coat with a red cross embroidered on the pouch. He looked old, as if he could have been the model for the dog in *Little Orphan Annie,* the 1940s newspaper comic strip. I've never seen anything like this animal in a white coat. I am ignorant of dog breeds with Mississippi Choctaw ancestral pedigrees. She said that the pouch contained seizure medication, a syringe, and needle.

The Catahoula is muzzled. He looked up at me with distressed glassy eyes and I assumed that his seizures were so often that he would bite off his tongue unless constantly medicated. I felt terrible. No animal should have to wear medication strapped to its body. I flashed to a scene I remembered from the sci-fi film *Dune* where a dog and cat are surgically sewn together and a bad actor has to milk the dog-cat to get enough antibiotic to inject himself daily in order to stay alive. Strange segue I know, but that's what I thought of. I grimaced at the dog owner, showing all my teeth, just like I think the dog would—if it could. What kind of a person makes a Choctaw dog suffer like this? She should just put him down.

My family would never allow the poor thing to live on in such misery and I blurt this out to the woman.

Turns out, it was the woman that had seizures. The Catahoula is a "service dog." He's trained to signal passersby that his owner is having a seizure. Pedestrians are then supposed to take the syringe out of the dog's pouch and shoot up Edith. (The 70s really had a profound influence on my generation.) By now, people around me were tittering. Even the Catahoula was embarrassed. I would like to say that I turned red in the face but then again, I'm always red-faced. I *am* after all a Choctaw with a long distinguished pedigree in Mississippi, just like the dog.

Then a few weeks later, May 22, 2002, at exactly 5 P.M., I was taken hostage by a cranky Asian bus driver in San Francisco on my way back from giving a reading from my new book at DQ University in Northern California. I think the bus driver was Japanese, but because I was unable to get his name, I can only lump together three quarters of humanity and just say he was "Asian." Which is like saying that all 550 or so tribes are one big Native American group. Not to mention the indigenous natives in Central and South Americas.

Being kidnapped was the "last straw" in a series of events, which likely caused my sudden weight loss. A friend of mine, anthropologist Raymond Fogelson[1], writes about the uses of categorizing events in understanding memory and histories. He says, "As minimal units in historical discourse, events must be described, analyzed, ordered, and interpreted." Ray goes on to consider a short list of event and non-event categories that includes "pseudo-events," in which everyone agrees something happened, but they disagree about its significance; the imagined event, one that never happened but *should have* happened; and finally the epitomizing event that condenses, encapsulates, and dramatizes longer-term historical processes that also affect human memories.

Back to the bus and pseudo-events.

Once I arrived in San Francisco, I bought a roundtrip train ticket from Oakland to Davis. When I'd returned to Oakland, I

was supposed to take AC Transit back to Embarcadero, where
two women from my publisher's office would pick me up and
drive me to another reading that same evening.

Already I'm worried about being late when we get across
the bay and I see the traffic. Thank goodness Karl Malden and
Michael Douglas aren't trying to film their action-packed TV
series "Streets of San Francisco" in the twenty-first century.
Today's public thoroughfares look like a giant parking lot. It just
couldn't happen.

But even without the traffic, the cranky Asian bus driver
was able to hold us hostage for forty-five minutes (in stop and
go traffic) because we'd all seen the movie *Die Hard* and suffered
from the Stockholm syndrome. In other words, as good liberals
and well-educated people, most of us identified with the bus
driver and worker's rights, and of course we all knew what had
happened to the Japanese Americans during WWII. At least
everyone but the "Greatest Generation" crowd sitting at the back
of the bus.

It all started when our bus driver said he's had enough of
the AARPers in the back complaining about the "so-called
discounted bus tickets for senior citizens." He drove us around
and around and kept deliberately passing Market Street where
the elderly people wanted to go. And he said he wouldn't stop
the bus until his demands were met.

"Not until I get a 'sincere' apology from those in the back of
the bus for their bad behavior and bad words."

Because I am Choctaw, and because I am from a tribal
society, and I've had a great deal of experience with commu-
nicating the efficacy of pseudo-events, I stood up as the bus
was circling the streets of San Francisco, and apologized for all
AARP members, *and* their voting patterns in the 2000 presiden-
tial election, and for the United States government for putting
Japanese-Americans in internment camps during WWII. I also
said that while I did not yet belong to the AARP, cultural anthropologists like Raymond Fogelson would label my relation-

ship with the elderly as "fictive kinship" (I would be turning 49 next year) enabling me to make the apology for the entire AARP organization.

The cranky Asian bus driver would have none of it. He ordered me to stop talking.

"Sit down little big woman." Later, I note in my diary that Asians are as full of clichés as American Indians. "Be quiet or I'll drive back onto the Oakland Bridge and into the freezing waters of the bay." At that point, I began to compose a farewell letter.

My dearest, most beloved family,

Please know that I died honorably, fighting social injustices wherever I encountered them—even on a sorry AC Transit bus."

Love to all.

Finally a dapper old lady wearing a Buster Brown hat and carrying a fuchsia-colored umbrella said she was "sincerely sorry" for the yelling and calling our cranky Asian bus driver bad names, like *Yellow Peril, Charlie Chan,* and *Mr. Susie Wong.* (Everyone is so dead earnest in San Francisco.) But it worked. No sooner had the words left her mouth than our bus rolled to a stop. Once before I had heard about the power of the word "sincerely," from a Christian missionary for her bad treatment of Native children at kindergarten school. Perhaps it was the ancient Latin word (*sincerus*) itself that had mythical powers. At any rate, the bus driver must have felt the full force of the word "sincerely" because he set us free. As I was running to the Market Street stop, already late of course, I couldn't help wondering if President George W. Bush shouldn't have tried using this word to quell Al Queda's rage against America. "I *sincerely* ask you to stop killing us." Who knows, it might have worked better than bombs.

Being held hostage for three-quarters of an hour maybe wouldn't have been so bad, except earlier the same day a cab driver in Davis had refused to drive me to Deganawidah-Quetzalcoatl University, also known as DQ University.

DQ is the all-Indian university that Nixon promised to build if the American Indian college students, their families, and urban Indians would relinquish Alcatraz Island in 1971. Natives held Alcatraz Island for eighteen months, from Nov. 20, 1969, until June 11, 1971, reclaiming it as "Indian land" when it was abandoned by the Feds, who rarely, if ever, practice due diligence where Indigenous people are concerned.

Today DQ looks like a series of abandoned school cafeterias from the Eisenhower era. There is one dusty road in and out of the "complex." The concrete block buildings are painted varying shades of baby-shit yellow. (There is only so much that can be done with bad materials.) What Indians learn in Indian kinder-garten... is that the FEDS love to stack concrete blocks and lock us inside. All Indian reservations were once renovated by stacking concrete blocks into what is laughingly called HUD housing. The FEDS seemed to have forgotten that concrete blocks require cement to glue them together. In a matter of days, the blocks began to fall down. Everywhere you look on reservations and in American Indian communities are stubs of concrete houses and concrete stores. Stubs of squalor. Monuments to the FEDS, and to BIA officials who pass out federal housing contracts to fat cat political donors of the party in power. There has always been a harmonious understanding between the two political parties when it comes to American Indians. We are the ones who get reamed. It's simply more democratic for both parties to have a go at us.

But, I digress. Back to the cab driver in Davis.

At the train station I leaned into a taxi window and asked the cabby to take me to DQ University. He looked me up and down, thought about my request, and then sped away. I ran after him in heels, carrying my briefcase hollering. "Hey, come back here!"

A woman driving a 1967 Chevy Impala zipped alongside of me. "Get in! I saw what happened," she shouted. "Men are so hostile!" As if I were a stuntwoman in a *Lethal Weapon* movie,

I jumped into her car, she put the pedal to the medal, and we burned rubber all the way down the road.

Under normal circumstances I am not a stupid woman. I am thoughtful; except for the time in 1968 I wanted to vote for Richard Nixon because he said he would end the war in Vietnam. But I was too young to vote so that doesn't count. As I studied my savior, who was driving like hell, swerving in and out, around BMWs, cyclists, and joggers, I realized that she was indeed a hippie, raging against the industries of war.

I could see she was once, no doubt, a trendy California girl with lustrous long blond hair. She'd probably listened to psychedelic rock, embraced the sexual revolution, and used drugs like cannabis and LSD to explore alternative states of consciousness. Now she's the granny at the local Health Food Store who turns to you while she's adding up your bill and says, "Prescription drugs are for pussies."

Skinny, dressed in shorts and sandals, her long hair is now streaked with gray and pulled back into a ponytail. She's smoking like a nervous bank robber, but given her age, I chalked it up to fluctuating hormones. I couldn't have chosen a more suspicious-looking stranger to get in a car with. But I was desperate. The reading at DQ was scheduled to begin in twenty minutes, and I am an unknown Choctaw author in San Francisco-land.

"Where to?" she barked.

"DQ University. I'm a writer and—"

"Where?" she shouted. I should mention that the engine was whining loudly and smoke was coming from under the hood.

"DQ University."

"Never heard of it, honey." She gripped her cigarette between her teeth, ground the gears down into second, and sped around a Volvo. "Goddamn yuppies." Then yelling out the window, "Drive it or park it, asshole!"

I hadn't heard the word "Yuppie" applied to a Volvo driver since 1989. It was then I realized my savior's pupils were tiny, the size of needlepoints. The skin around her nostrils was reddish and swollen and she seemed—well, kinda strung out. I was crestfallen because I knew then that I wasn't going to make it to the reading. Perhaps ever.

"A school, huh?"

"Yeah, it's in Yolo County on Road 31. About 7 miles west of California State Route 113."

She hit the brakes. We came to a screeching halt. Thank goodness I had a good deal of practice at "riding defensively." I'd once lived in the Middle East where I learned to keep my briefcase on my lap when riding with Egyptian cabbies who had perfected the art of "disaster braking." What I'd learned is that a briefcase protects you from the windshield. Of course, it also helps to be dead drunk so you won't notice when your taxi collides with goats, sheep, chickens, donkeys, and other Arab pedestrians. Luckily, the Volvo behind us slammed on its brakes, barely missing us by an inch.

"I can't take you out there! You have to get out of my car," she screamed.

"Right here?"

"I'm sorry."

I began to plead. "Can't you drop me at some busy street corner, instead of here?"

She took a long drag of her cigarette and waved to the driver of the Volvo. "Go around," she roared. "Jesus!" After a few seconds she said, "I've got it. Firemen help people. I'll take you to a fire station and they'll know what to do."

She had trouble starting the car, but eventually we were once again whipping in and out of traffic just as before. She looked over at me and lowered her voice, conspiratorially. "When we get there, let me do all the talking. I know just what to say."

As a rule of thumb, there are two ways to handle this. First, never try to figure out what's going to happen next. You'll scare yourself. Second, it's important to have your facts straight before you race into a fire station with a cokehead. Law enforcement personnel, and by association firemen, do not want to waste time while you try to work out a plausible story.

Amazingly, within a few minutes she'd actually found a fire station. She jumped out of the car and ran into the building screaming, "Help!" This time I was a bit quicker on my feet. I made a mad dash into the building. The firefighters looked at us as if we were both cokeheads, but I managed to calmly interrupt her story. Apparently I convinced them that I was mostly sane, because the fire chief, a tall well-built blonde originally from the Netherlands (age 35, height 6'4" 185 pounds) instructed his secretary to call me a cab. Unfortunately my savior made a quick exit before I could get her name and thank her. The fire chief offered me a hotdog and some fries, and I must say we had a nice exchange about the benefits of added calcium in today's milk products. He claimed he was health-conscious and looking for a woman who was equally concerned about her body. (I let him know that I was.) We also traded phone numbers and email addresses, promising to keep in touch, yet I didn't expect to hear from him. But I gave him a copy of my book, anyway.

A taxi arrived almost immediately; the fire chief's brother owned a cab company in Davis. The rest of the ride to DQ University was uneventful. I was an hour late for my scheduled reading at DQ, but the American Indian students hadn't given up. They are accustomed to visitors arriving late. When I walked in they were still seated in the assembly room, waiting patiently. They had prepared a list of questions about the history of Choctaws and the tribes from the southeastern United States. The Native students were from all across California. One young woman, a Modoc, said she was going to college to become a lawyer. Another girl was Pomo and from a basket-making family. She said she wanted to make documentary films about the tribes in the Amazon. They were an amazing group of students, and I even got to see my friend Jack Forbes who was teaching at DQ.

Then on the last day of the book tour in San Francisco, my publisher rented a room in the Women's Building in the Mission

District to host a press party for my book. A non-Indian woman named Shirley (not her real name) brought her play for me to read to the guests. When I begged off, she and a group of other women performed the story of a Cherokee prostitute who owned a brothel in San Francisco. It burned down in the 1890s, killing the indigenous prostitute and all her customers. A kind of comedy of errors. During the play's performance, I did the only thing I could do. I downed four or five glasses of red wine. One after another.

Amazingly, I was still upright by the time it was my turn to say a few words about my book and *uh-hem*, read. Shortly afterwards a group of Lesbian-Buddhist-activists forced us to relinquish the room for their regular Friday night meditation. A friend helped me to his car and we proceeded to a Korean bar where we had *Soju Slushes*, a kind of alcohol made from fermented sweet potatoes blended with fruit and ice. *Truly*, a San Francisco version of a multi-cultural experience.

The next day, suffering from a terrible hangover and feeling morose, I was back on the road for the final stop on the book tour. My publisher had arranged for me to give a reading in San Jose, California, but first I needed food, and lots of it.

The Peruvian restaurant downtown was cozy and filled with the aroma of chili peppers and savory quinoa. A black man sat down next to my table, took one look at me and said, *"Chi niah katimi?"*

At last, a voice from home! Someone who knows our language. *"Keyu,"* not good, I replied.

"Say, didn't we meet in Japan, or was it Jordan? No wait, it was Jerusalem?"

I smiled, but said, "I don't believe we've met before. I think I would have remembered."

"Choctaws are born adventurers," he said, motioning for the waitress. "Our memories, whether clumsy or discreet, are woven into the fabric of *okchamali*. Life. I was there all right. I can see we're going to have to put some meat on your bones."

"What do you suggest?" I asked.

"I'd start with a plate of tamales wrapped in banana leaves with a side of boiled potatoes, beans, and corn."

"Sounds perfect."

I glanced around to look for the waitress. When I turned back the man had disappeared and a steaming plate of food was sitting on the table.

Typical.

Notes

1 Raymond D. Fogelson, "The Ethnohistory of Events and Nonevents," *Ethnohistory*, Vol. 36, No. 2 (Duke U P,: Spring, 1989), pp. 133-147.

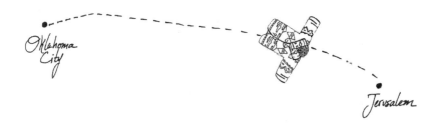

Oklahoma City

Jerusalem

Choctalking on Other Realities

There is only one pigeon left in Jerusalem. It could be the weather. Perhaps his more clever relatives took refuge in the cities by the Red Sea where the climate is better. Jerusalem occupies a high plateau in Israel/Palestine. In January 1992, record snows have fallen here. Outside our hotel, ice-covered oranges weigh the trees down like leaded Christmas ornaments.

I've come to Israel/Palestine as an academic tourist on a university-sponsored tour. We're told that with few natural advantages and no indigenous raw materials, apart from stone, the economy of Jerusalem has always been supported from the outside. They're entirely dependent on peace. If that's true, we want to know why Jews, Muslims, and Christians in Jerusalem have adopted the stance of a "mobilized society." Perhaps it's their heritage. Each of these religious groups has always made great sacrifices to change the status quo. Recall the Jews taking Canaan and greater Israel; the Christians capturing the Roman Empire and the New World; and the Muslims seizing Arabia, Asia, and Africa. The wars of heaven.

I leave the National Palace Hotel in East Jerusalem and meander down a narrow street. The pigeon comes and goes. He sails above my head. I pass a park where the benches are vacant and gray. As the afternoon light creeps behind another ragged wall of snow clouds I stop. The bird lands just beyond my reach, and I throw him the remains of my falafel sandwich. A late breakfast. We eye each other until he draws his head back as if his attention is fixed in the distance on something no one else sees. Eventually I see it too. A group of women march toward us chanting slogans in Arabic and the sky cracks open and the pigeon flies away.

They're Palestinians. Seven women. Their arms are linked together in solidarity like a chain of paper dolls. I don't understand what they are saying but I can guess. They want to change the status quo.

I follow the procession. After all, this is what I've come for. To see who is doing what to whom. Like peeping toms or UN observers, we academics do very little except tell each other what we've seen. Always in dead earnest.

Soon tourists come out of the shops to see what all the ruckus is about. The women encourage us to join their protest. In a few minutes two blue and white truckloads of soldiers arrive carrying white clubs and tear gas launchers. The women stay together as long as they can until they are broken apart by the soldiers. Many of the tourists become frantic. They run into the soldiers or away from them. People scramble in all directions.

One woman breaks away from the others and runs in the direction of the American Colony Hotel. For some unexplainable reason I run after her.

Suddenly she's behind me. I know her by the sound of her feet running. I run faster across the dirt playground. If she catches me I'll never escape. I hear her panting loudly. Her weight and large frame knocks me down. I can't breathe. Her blonde face blushes red as she yanks me up by my arms.

I twist out of her grasp and run toward a fence made of chicken wire. Beyond it is the WA-HE Café in Bethany, Oklahoma. Indians are inside drinking coffee and gossiping about the weather. If I make it to the WA-HE they'll protect me. But she tackles me again. Hammers my head with her elbow. Sweat pours out of her body and wets my face. I gag trying not to swallow. A second white teacher comes to her aid. Together they carry me toward a small building, the kindergarten school connected to their church. They open the broom closet and shove me inside. The door slams shut.

I am still running.

This Is the Story I Really Wanted to Tell

It was so hot in the kitchen of the Oklahoma City airport café that the plastic clock melted. Time oozed down the wall just like Salvador Dalí imagined. The metal pieces of the flimsy clock went, "clink, clank, ting" as they hit the floor. That's because the steaks were burning, the beans were boiling, and Nina the Ukrainian had pulled a butcher knife on Gretchen the German. There is a war going on. I am in uniform. But I race ahead of myself. This story begins in 1970.

First there are the characters.

Gretchen the German. A Catholic. The blonde cook with the white hairnet pulled down over her ears like a helmet. A Berliner, she escaped Nazi Germany during World War II to come to America and cook wiener schnitzels. That's what she tells all the customers at the airport café.

Susan B. Anthony. The black, six-foot-tall-night-cook-in-charge, Susan B. likes the blues. Speaks choicest Gullah. Cooks like snapping fingers in time. Her great-great-grandmother was a slave. Every night at the airport café she says, "Honey, don't mess with me." And I don't.

Nina. A Russian Jew from the Ukraine, she wears a white cotton uniform with socks held up by rubber bands. Nina's thumb is tattooed and causes people to stare impolitely. She says she escaped the massacre at Babi Yar. Each night she chisels perfect heads of lettuce into identical salads and weighs each portion. She is quite insane.

And me. An Oklahoma Choctaw. The waitress in the yellow uniform at the airport café. I'm a union steward for the International Brotherhood of Hotel, Motel, and Restaurant Workers of America; I'm nineteen years old and have been baptized many times. The Southern Baptists, the Nazarenes, even the Mormons got to me. Finally, I've given up being a religious consumer to become a socialist. The AFL-CIO is going to send me to college.

The Scene.

The airport café. Feeding time. The fall of 1970. Nightshift comes through the looking glass walls of the airport café. Braniff and United Airlines roar out of sight to exotic places. Somewhere a radio blasts Leon Russell's singing, "...*Here comes Uncle Sam again with the same old bag of beans. Local chiefs on the radio, we got some hungry mouths to feed, goin' back to Alcatraz.*"

At 6:30 P.M., one hundred Vietnam draftees drag into the Oklahoma City airport café. Afros, pork-chop sideburns, crew cuts, Indian braids. After two years, hairless pimpled faces all look alike. Some smell bad. Some have beautiful teeth.

It's not news at the airport café that the Vietnam War is being fought disproportionately by the poor. Every Monday through Friday we serve red and yellow, black, and poor white boys their last supper as civilians. They're on their way to boot camp. They clutch their government orders and puke-belch to themselves. Their hands shake. My hands are steady. I want to tell them to run. But don't.

"*No one gets hurt if they do what they're told,*" whispered the white teacher through the door of the broom closet. "*Would you like to come out now?*"

"Curious," booms a voice across the airport café's dining room. Some of the draftees look toward the kitchen, others continue eating as if they'd heard nothing.

The voice gathers strength and explodes.

"There were no survivors of Babi Yar," roars Gretchen grimly.

I rush through the kitchen door. The steaks are burning, and the beans are boiling over the fire, and Gretchen is scrutinizing Nina in front of the gas grill.

"Your story is certainly unfamiliar to me. You probably branded your own thumb so people won't accuse you. Very clever."

Nina's eyes make a circle of the kitchen. She examines her work; the stainless steel bins of freshly washed lettuce, tomatoes, radish flowers, onions, carrots, and watermelon balls. All are arranged, lined up in neat rows at her workstation. "I do what I am told," she says pushing her head against the walk-in freezer. "The sins of my occupation."

"What a wreck you are. Always building a pile of shadows," says Gretchen grabbing a slice of onion.

Nina's mouth is set in a fold of bitterness. "I know Babi Yar. It's a ravine near Kiev where the Germans murdered 35,000 Jews in September 1941. By 1943, it had become a mass grave for more than 100,000 Jews." She looks at something beyond us then screams. "I WAS THERE!"

"Yes, but what did you do?"

Nina charges Gretchen with a butcher knife in one hand, and a watermelon scoop in the other. Gretchen holds a small toaster oven in front of her like a shield. Together they dance around the room like a couple of marionettes being pulled by the fingers of God.

Eventually Susan B. Anthony interrupts the madness and Gretchen shouts, "SCHWEIG, du Neger!"

This is where I come in. I intercede like a good union steward should. Susan B. Anthony holds a hot pan of grease and is set to attack them both. The World War II survivors are screaming in languages I can't understand and pointing their weapons. They all scare the hell out of me because I'm unarmed.

1970 is a terrible year to be a teenage Indian in Oklahoma City. Vietnam is on television, nightly. World War II is still going on in the kitchen of the airport café, and I'm losing my classmates to mortar fire in Asia. Emmet Tahbone is dead. Blown away, literally. Richard Warrior is MIA, and George Billy has a shrapnel mouth.

This past week there were sit-ins at a downtown department store where blacks are still being refused services at the lunch counter. For almost ten months American Indians have occupied the abandoned prison on Alcatraz Island. The word on the streets of Oklahoma City is that we're fed up with colonialism. American Indians are finally going to change the status quo. Standing in the middle of the kitchen with my palms turned upward, a sign that I carry no weapons, I squint like a mourner who draws the curtains against the light. I feel powerless to change anything.

I look out the window and a moonbeam is crisscrossing a watery plain. It's the Pearl River with its saw grass islands and Cypress knees rising out of the water like hands in prayer to Hashtali, whose eye is the Sun. This light once cut clear across the heavens and down to the Choctaw's ancient mother mound, the Nanih Waiya in the Lower Mississippi Valley. Now it's no longer visible except on special occasions.

I see a Choctaw woman, her daughter, and their relatives. They're being attacked by a swarm of warriors from another tribe. Unfortunately bad weather has driven them into a little bayou. They're exposed from head to foot to their enemies, the Cherokees, who've been following them for days. The Choctaw woman shows her daughter how to be brave. Several times she runs and cuts the powder horns loose from her dead relatives in order to distribute them among the living. Finally the seven warriors, and the mother and daughter, seeing that they can no longer hold their ground rush headlong upon their enemies.

A feminine voice interrupts my vision. *"No one gets hurt if they do what they're told."* I shake my head, trying to drive it out of me. *"We fly daily non-stop flights to locations across America,*

Europe, and Asia," continues the recorded message on the airport's loudspeaker.

I turn back to my co-workers, who are drowning in a pool of tears. "No one will get hurt if we do what we're supposed to do," I say meekly. For a moment no one moves. Then they begin struggling with their kitchen utensils. Suddenly Nina is composed, Gretchen too, both of them square their shoulders the way soldiers do when called to attention. They promise it will never happen again, but no one believes them.

At midnight the lines on my face have melted like the clock in Salvador Dalí's painting. I resemble a sad clown. When Susan B. Anthony and I walk outside to share a smoke we eye one another warily.

"What happened?" I ask quietly.

"God knows," she says lighting a cigarette.

Together we watch as the lights of a crayon-colored Braniff jet leave a trail of stale dead air, and I think I'll buy a mask and become someone else. The AFL-CIO can't save me now.

Choctalking on Other Realities

I did become someone else. A mother, a teacher, a writer, a wife. When the opportunity came to visit Israel in 1992, I signed up for the two-week trip at the behest of my husband, a geographer and co-leader of the study tour. We are going to Jerusalem to learn about the effects of the Intifada on the region and its peoples. At first, I was hesitant. The very word Jerusalem connotes religion. Three of them: Judaism, Christianity, Islam, birthed in that order. They all look the same to me. They share one God known as Yahweh, Allah, or Jesus. They honor the same prophets. They share many of the same books. Their holidays center around religious and cultural victories over each other. Kind of like Americans celebrating Thanksgiving. Holidays are the masks of conquerors.

But wouldn't you know it. On my first day in Jerusalem I met a Jewish woman who said her great-grandmother was a Cherokee.

She tells me it is a long story—how one side of her family immigrated to America, then re-immigrated to Israel after 1948. I stand motionless and look at the woman across the glass counter of her gift shop. Listen skeptically to the ragged tenderness of her story. The weary but elusive Indian ancestry, the fawning desire to be related to me, at least my Indianness, is something I've experienced before.

I study the shopkeeper's face. We are remarkably alike. Black eyes. Dark hair. About the same age. As the shadows of Jerusalem invade her shop windows I grow nostalgic. The city looms under a delicious haze of smoke from the outdoor falafel stands, and I want to take this woman away with me. To cross time and the ocean together. To place her in our past, to put myself in her beginning, and intertwine our threads of history—for we are nothing without our relationships. That's Choctaw.

I begin my story in the middle. "Choctaws are not originally from Oklahoma. We are immigrants too."

The woman whose ancestor was a Cherokee nods her head as if she understands, and I continue.

"Our ancient homelands are in the Southeastern part of the United States where we were created in the spectacular silken flatness of the delta lands. The earth opened her body and beckoned us to join her above ground so our ancestors tunneled up through her navel into tinges of moist red men and women. We collected our chins, knees, breasts, and sure-footed determination—long before Moses parted the Red Sea, and the God with three heads was born in the Middle East.

"Choctaws were the second largest allied group of peoples in the Southeast. Our population centers were clustered like wheels around three major rivers: to the east the Tombigbee River; to the west the Pearl River; and in the South the Chickasawhay River. We made trading relationships with other tribes in our regions whenever possible."

She interrupts my story, asks me if I will come to her house for an evening meal. She talks on. Says that she went to school in New York City, and that she misses the company of Americans. Her own mother is dead, since she was a child. All she has left is her father, the one who owns the shop. She looks at me. "You promise to tell me more of your history?"

"What I can."

Her home is west of Jerusalem. Opposite the old city where everyone walks instead of rides. There are great American-style streets full of Mercedes, Peugeots and Perrier bottles. Her place is elegant, an estate on a hill. There's a dark studio with a mahogany desk, Navajo rugs, and an enormous basket made from the skeleton of a Saguaro tree sits near the stone fireplace. She builds a fire against the cold and opens the shutters to let in the city. She says she doesn't feel anything in particular toward the Arabs, no hate, and no repulsion either. I asked her what about the Choctaws? She smiles, not knowing what I mean. She says she is where she has to be. Placed here. Of course she feels a tinge of fear. It's as if this is not only what she expects, but what must happen to her.

She says she pays closest attention to the noise of the city. That the city shouts what is going to happen. The explosions, the bullets, the prayers, the celebratory demonstrations, they're all part of it she says, like messages from God.

She begins telling me some rigmarole about how Jerusalem meets the needs of all its people. Throughout its four-thousand-year history she says the city was meant to be a place of unity. Her father believes that now the Intifada is over there can be peace between the Arabs and Jews.

Behind her a shadow walks into the room. I see the image of a woman in darned socks. I think I recognize her face, but I can't quite make it out, so speak up without waiting for a polite pause in our conversation.

"Then why, every day, do Jews and Arabs try and kill one another?"

"Why did Indians sell Manhattan to the Christians?"

Night comes through the shutters. The din of the streets below grows louder. It's more penetrating than the livid red streetlamps.

We look at each other. Our expressions are suddenly changed. We realize we're on the side of societies that have reduced us to grief.

All the same she rushes to tell me the story of her great-grandfather, a shoemaker, an outcast in North Carolina just like her great-grandmother, the Cherokee. "He was in exile, she was conquered. They fell in love because they had this in common. After World War II my grandfather, the one who was half-Jewish-half-Cherokee, made a pilgrimage to the Holy Land. He never returned to America."

"Indians are not conquered!"

"But your nerve is gone," she says, sadly. "I was a student at New York City University when the Indians surrendered Alcatraz Island in June 1971. We would have never given up."

There is a long silence.

"Who is we?" I ask.

"I've provoked you," she says. "Now I give you the chance to give me a piece of your mind."

There is a trace of something odd in her remark, so I begin with a metaphor. "Once a very ancient god came back from everywhere. Arriving at a banquet in his honor with a bundle of keys, he announced that it was closing time, and toilets around the world exploded."

We laugh. It breaks the tension.

"It's from the good book. The missing pages."

"And then what happened?" she asks. "You promised to tell me your history."

"After the war ended between the British and the French in 1763 Indians in the Southeast couldn't make the foreigners do anything. Soldiers went AWOL and married into our tribes. No one wanted to live in Paris or London anymore. That's why so many Choctaws, Creeks, Chickasaws, and Cherokees have

British and French last names.

"In 1830, after the Treaty of Dancing Rabbit Creek was signed, the Choctaw are the first to be removed from our ancient homelands. Many walked all the way with very little to eat or drink. The road to the Promised Land was terrible. Dead horses and their dead riders littered the way. Dead women lay in the road with babies dried to their breasts, tranquil as if napping. A sacred compost for scavengers."

She stokes the fire to keep it from dying, and I know the more revolting the details, the less she believes me. Finally she says, "You are exaggerating."

"Perhaps. But four thousand Choctaws died immigrating to Oklahoma."

"It is late," she says, ignoring my facts. "Time I returned you to your hotel. I'm sure your husband is waiting for you."

"But you said you wanted to know about my history?"

She gives me a fishy look but agrees. "Very well."

"It's no accident that there are sixty-six Indian Nations head-quartered in Oklahoma. Oklahoma or Indian Territory was a forerunner of Israel. Choctaws were the first to be removed there, other Indian tribes from around the country soon followed. We were supposed to live together in peace. Form relationships. It wasn't easy, but for the most part we did it because we do not idealize war. However throughout the nineteenth century more and more whites moved into Indian Territory. Followed by missionaries and lawyers who began converting us, or swindling us."

"Then on April 22, 1889 the American government opened the unassigned lands to the whites. When the trumpet sounded, the Run of 1889 began. It was estimated that twenty thousand immigrants were waiting at the border to stake their claims. Today the Run of 1889 is an annual celebration in Oklahoma. Like a holiday."

"I thought you were going to tell me *your* story."

"I'm coming to it," I answer, pausing to clear my throat. "There was no color in the broom closet. Light edged around the door. There may have been other teachers outside the closet, but I only knew of her by the smell of her sweat.

"The church had started a kindergarten program. She was a missionary. That morning the preacher said we were lucky to have a missionary lead us in a song. *"Red and yellow, black and white, we are separate in his sight, Jesus loves the little children of the world."* Then I sang it several times by myself. I was only repeating what I thought I heard. The words had no meaning for me, I was five years old. When she marched toward me shaking her fist, with that mouth of angry nails I panicked and ran outside across the playground and toward a café.

"Down, down, down, the fall crushes me, and I'm mucking around in the dirt. She oozed through my pores that hot afternoon in Bethany, Oklahoma, and there she has remained whispering inside my head."

I stare at my host. "It isn't that we lost our nerve. Sometimes we're just overwhelmed."

After I finish my story, a strange quiet grips the Jewish woman whose ancestor was a Cherokee. Her face becomes attentive, as if listening to something that penetrated her soul.

When she drops me off at the National Palace Hotel, I watch her drive away. All I can think of is that she's right, that Jerusalem, "the city of peace," is what is meant to happen to her.

There Is No God but God

The next day I rejoin our study tour and we meet some Palestinian women from the Gaza Strip. In 1992 the Gaza Strip is still one of the Occupied Territories of Israel. The Palestinian women tell us their stories through an interpreter. One woman says that the government prohibits them from displaying the colors of the Palestinian flag, which are green, red, black, and white. She says her husband has been arrested for having a picture of a watermelon on his desk. Many others show us empty tear-gas canisters that have been shot into their homes by the soldiers. They are plainly marked, "MADE IN USA."

To show concern for the Palestinians some members of our study tour present the women with duffel bags full of used clothes and high heel shoes marked MADE IN USA. I didn't bring any used clothes, so I ask the Christian coordinator from the Council of Middle East Churches if I could give the Palestinian women money instead of used clothes.

"No," she replies. "They'll just come to expect it from us."

The next day when the study tour leaves for a two-day visit to Nazareth, I stay behind at our hotel. I've had enough. I want to be alone, walk the streets of the old city, and eat in the small cafés.

Throughout the day prayers are broadcast over loud-speakers. For Muslims, the first prayer of the day begins at the moment the rays of the sun begin to appear on the horizon. The last prayer in the evening ends at sunset. Devout Jews pray three times a day; devout Muslims pray five times daily. When I hear a man singing the prayers on a mosque's loud speaker system I am sure he is praying to the Sun, just like Choctaws once prayed to Hashtali.

"The prayers are to Allah, not the Sun," says a vendor outside the Al-Aqsa Mosque in Jerusalem.

"It looks like you are praying to the Sun, especially with your palms turned up toward the sky. The Egyptians once worshipped the sun God, Ra. Since the Hebrews and the Egyptians once lived together, maybe your religions rubbed off on each other. Everyone in this country says 'Yis-RA-el' for Israel. Maybe there's a relationship?"

He waved me away. "No, no, no, you have been misinformed! There is no God, but the God of us all."

I Am Still Running

Palestinian men from around the community race past me toward the soldiers and meet them head-on. The protest explodes into a riot. Mothers, daughters, and grandmothers from inside the shops join the women in the streets. The soldiers begin dragging people inside the blue and white paddy wagons, one or two at a time, amidst weeping and bleeding fists.

I run toward the leader crumpled against the stone wall. Suddenly I recognize her. It's Nina from the airport café. I can't believe it, but it's really Nina. She's dressed in her white cotton uniform, her shabby socks still held up with rubber bands. A soldier reaches her before me.

"Don't hurt her, it's Nina. Can't you see? She's a survivor of Babi Yar."

Suddenly I'm on the ground. I cannot breathe. Someone rifles through my purse and pulls out my American passport. He yanks me up by my arms and tells me in English to go home.

"No one gets hurt if they do what they're told."

"No, it's a lie. RUN!" I scream so loud that I frighten the voice out of my head.

Nina gets up and tries to jump the stone fence, but the soldier bashes her in the legs with a club. She falls down and he carries her to the paddy wagon and shoves her inside.

I am back to the dubious place where memory distorts fragments of an indivisible experience and we meet a different self. It wasn't Nina the soldier carried into the government vehicle. She died talking to God that terrible night in the airport café. She collapsed on the floor of the kitchen, not long after the fight with Gretchen, asking God why she had to die, why now that she'd regained her courage. "Very well," was all she whispered.

Standing in the middle of the street in East Jerusalem, I watch the determined faces of the Palestinian women and weep for Nina. I still believe she is with the Palestinian protesters, just as I believe she was at Babi Yar.

An Arab member of the Knesset, the Israeli parliament, finally arrives in a government car and calls for calm. He holds both hands out to the soldiers, a sign that he carries no weapons.

The pigeon returns and lands next to me, as if surveying the waste. The Knesset member sees us, stops, then walks on with his palms facing toward the Sun. I will believe the rest of my life that this is what he prayed for.

"Save her. She is the Jewish women shot to death by the Germans at Babi Yar.

"Save her. She is the Palestinian women shot to death by the Jews at Deir Yassin.

"Save her. She is the Vietnamese women shot to death by the Americans at Mi Lai.

"Save her. She is the Mayan women shot to death by the Mexicans in Chiapas.

"Save her. She is the Black women shot to death by the Ku Klux Klan in Alabama.

"Save her. She is The People, our grandmothers, our mothers, our sisters, our ancestors, ourselves.

"Save us."

Tokyo
Iowa
City
Okayama

I Fuck Up in Japan

The first time I experienced a heated toilet seat was in Okayama City, Japan, February 1993. Some cross-cultural experiences do not easily translate into words; using a heated toilet seat may be one of them. It was my first trip to the Far East. Before I completed the three-week tour, giving lectures to Japanese groups and visiting with local dignitaries in towns and cities, I would have diverse experiences with all manner of toilets and washing apparatuses associated with the o-furo, the Japanese bath.

I'd been invited to Japan as an American Indian representative to speak at the International Forum on Anti-Discrimination and Human Rights during the 1993 United Nations "International Year of the World's Indigenous People." (A mouthful, but it was serious business.) The plan was for me to do homestays with local host families throughout Japan and learn about their culture and the landscape. Ditto for the Japanese: they would learn about me.

My tribe was once bullish on homestays. In the eighteenth century, Choctaws were awash in foreigners, the French, the

Alsatians, the Germans, the Swiss, the Irish, the Scots, the occasional Spaniard, a menacing Englishman roaming here and there, all doing immersive family experiments in our homelands. Historic homestays were intended as a kind of tourism allowing for the sharing of cultures, lifeways, and experiences between different peoples from different lands. I know, *I know*, it didn't work out for Choctaws or other American Indian tribes, but since this was the end of the twentieth century, I hoped for a better outcome.

I prepared myself for investigating the cultural spine of Japan with exploratory questions (in English) such as, "How do you live?" "What is your work?" "Where is the bathroom?" In return I would reveal what I know of my own cultural anatomy. "I am Choctaw, an American Indian from the United States." "Yes, perhaps I do carry the genes of other heredity ancestors, our ancient mothers took homestays seriously." "Of course you may try on my red beaded warrior coat." "Remarkable. The coat does make you look just like an American Indian, although it's two sizes too big."

Japan is comprised of thousands of green islands and dormant and active volcanoes such as the majestic Mount Fuji, the highest mountain in the country, which I would visit after the forum ended. Rolling green hills flank the coastline, long and varied with hundreds of inland bays and natural harbors. I had a month to prepare for my trip to Japan but wasted a fair amount of time writing chapter titles for a travel book I would write. "My Travels in the Land of the Rising Sun." "An American Indian amongst the Samurai." "Sushi or Whale Blubber: Why I Chose Whale." (The last chapter was bound to get the attention of the environmentalists. Controversy sells.) All this was absolute lunacy. I should have spent my time learning Japanese. I didn't know a single word when I agreed to do the lectures. Of course I carried a journal with me that had a few words spelled out phonetically:

Ohayo gozaimasu: Good morning.

Konnichiwa: Good day.

Konbanwa: Good evening.

Oyasumi nasai: Good night.

Honno o shirushi de gozai masu ga: It only amounts to
a symbol of my appreciation.

Sama: Gives praise to the one who makes the meal.

Itadakimasu: I humbly receive.

Note that these words are responses to polite conversational
banter. I'd also foolishly written out a few sentences that I could
read aloud if asked about my family. Rare was the opportunity,
however, when I could bow properly, hold my journal in one
hand, and read the correct words at just the right time. I'd been
taught how to bow like a woman by a male Japanese professor
at the University of Iowa, where I was working as a staff person
in International Education. I practiced several times in front of
a mirror and thought I was prepared for genteel interactions. So
far, so good.

During the first week in Japan, I stayed in hotels and was
hosted by Professor Mitzuhito Kanehara of Hosei University in
Tokyo. He spoke English in a soft voice that made me wonder
if all Japanese men converse with such gentle countenance.
Together we visited historic sites around Tokyo and traveled
to other cities to see Shinto shrines and the Pacific Ocean.
We also had one very intense conversation about American
Indian identity and which authors were being incorrectly
translated into Japanese as "Native." After eight days, he took
me to stay with my first host family in Okayama City, where
the human rights forum was to be held. (I'll return to that
incident later.)

So, my Japanese toilet event: A cold spell swept across the
entire country the night of my first homestay. Temps plummeted
below freezing. Most Japanese homes didn't have central heating
or air conditioning. In a normal February, a vent-free space
heater that rolled from room to room would be adequate to heat
an average house. But this wasn't an average February. At dusk,
heavy wet snow fell and continued throughout the night.

My host family and I communicated through body language and hand gestures. A smile was happiness, hands on the heart, expressed gratitude. I was assured in an official letter from the Buraku Liberation League, given to me by my hosts, that a translator was on his way the next day. He would accompany me the rest of my journey throughout Japan and translate my lectures. In the meantime I was on my own.

We went to bed early and my hosts shut off the space heater to conserve energy. By midnight I had to go to the bathroom. The marble tiled room was lovely, yet bitter as a tomb. I began peeling off the seven layers of clothing I'd worn to bed, including a red pair of Lands' End long johns. I noted the furry material covering the toilet seat while stripping off my clothes, but ignored it. Naked, I sat down, jumped up, and then panicked. Wires inside fur!

"I'm going to be electrocuted," I hissed. I flashed on an image of Elvis Presley sitting on the commode just before his ginormous bloated body dolloped onto the floor. "Oh god, I can't end up like that!"

The room was so frigid I could see my breath. I didn't know what to do. I'd never felt a woolly toilet seat cover before, let alone a woolly heating pad. My mind was a feverish tangle of questions. What if a loose wire gets…wet? What if the mishap carries enough current to shock my heart and in a split second I'm history, killed by gadgetry. Will my Native friends laugh at the irony? Will my loved ones angrily complain that I should never have traveled to Japan in the first place? While Presley died of an overdose from mixing ten kinds of pills into a lethal cocktail that would at last quench his thirst, I'd had no intoxicants since arriving at Narita International Airport in Tokyo. Not even beer or wine, just buckets of hot green tea. I ran my trembling hands through my hair and shivered. "Stop thinking about Elvis Presley," I said through clenched teeth. "All that's beside the freaking point. *I've got to go!*"

I closed my eyes. All I could see was a bare red body cupped beside an icy cold porcelain throne. An ode to modernity. A few more seconds passed. At last I opened my eyes. The toilet and I regarded one another. *"Konbanwa,"* I said softly. Then I bowed slowly as I'd been taught, sat down, and hoped *not* to die.

I did not die. What I won't know until much later is there will be many times during my travels across Japan that I will wish I were dead. I was out of my depth, out of my mind, using the wrong words, consistently acting on the wrong assumptions, making too many cross-cultural mistakes.

Oklahoma could not have prepared me for the Far East.

Mongolians "R" Us

For me there will never be another travel adventure like Japan. I was one of four guest speakers at the International Forum on Anti-Discrimination and Human Rights. It had been publicized all over Japan and the organizers were expecting hundreds of people to attend. One of the major sponsors of my trip was the Buraku Liberation Research Institute in Okayama. After the forum on human rights I was scheduled for more homestays with Burakumin people and travel to other cities to give lectures about contemporary American Indians in the US.

Probably about this time in the story I should confess I was feeling a bit haughty about being invited to Japan. In a way, I felt the Japanese were partially responsible for driving me out of the securities business and into the hands of a university position (at a greatly reduced salary). In my mind this visit was fate, recompense, providence. A strange and perverse way to think, but I had once been in the pay of Wall Street; one twisted sister. "The Street" is selfish, narcissistic, and ravenous, was always gobbling people whole, small and large corporations, other country's currencies, and sleep. Apparently I still carried this perversion.

By the mid-1980s Wall Street was in distress, reeling and convulsing over the import-export disparity which affected the value of the US dollar. Japan, a major exporter of goods to the United States, was cutting their own profit margins rather than raise the dollar prices of Nintendo, fax machines, Canon cameras, and Sony televisions to US consumers. In the last quarter of 1986, US imports of nonpetroleum products exceeded US exports of nonagricultural goods by 74 percent. This trend led to an ever-increasing absolute deficit. Everyone from President Ronald Reagan to Secretary of State James Baker III and Wall Street blamed the Japanese for the US economic woes. The deficit also forced our firm to trim its buy-low sell-high strategies.

The truth is I didn't need the President of the United States or even Wall Street to tell me how to think about the Japanese; I was predisposed to blame them by members of my own family. Two days after Pearl Harbor was destroyed, my Cherokee grandmother in Ada, Oklahoma, broke all her Japanese Blue Willow china, plate by plate. She pounded them into porcelain paste with a Sears and Roebuck claw hammer, all the while cursing a blue streak. My grandfather intervened and she spared the last two dinner plates. After her death we found them wrapped in an old newspaper at the bottom of a chest that was jumbled with WWII memorabilia. The faded headline read "Japanese Bomb Pearl Harbor." (It seems Grandmother was a committed nationalist.)

Let's see, where was I? Scary isn't it, how one narrative bleeds into another—from Wall Street to Ronald Reagan to Pearl Harbor to my grandmother's Japanese china. Back to those early days of 1985 on Wall Street, our morning briefings from the New York trading desk went something like this:

"Japanese led again yesterday."

"Industrial production in Japan beats expectation."

"Bullish sentiment among traders down for the third straight week."

"Totally unconfirmed chatter about Plaza Accord, the plan by G-5 nations to manipulate exchange rates by depreciating the US dollar relative to the Yen and Deutsche mark."

"Here are the talking points of the day …"

As soon as New York's lead analyst signed off, Ed Hardy, our Houston bond trader, would come on the squawk box and dump on the briefings with his pithy one liners:

"Goddamn Japs."

"Ah well, payback. Next time, next time."

"Hiroshima, mon amour?"

Some of you may be thinking that I should have stood up against the racist remarks of my co-worker, and you'd be right. But without realizing it, I'd slipped into solidarity with thieves, corseted all indignation.

There was another equally felonious reason I wanted to go to Japan. Owing to a poor education in the sixth grade in Oklahoma (my teacher also coached the junior high football team), I wanted to know if the Japanese believed they were related to American Indians. Mr. Bill (a white male) said, according to scientists, the Indians in Oklahoma were Mongols. This came as quite a surprise to my grandmother when I told her. "Mr. Bill says Indians are related to all Orientals." Grandmother raised her eyebrows and started to speak but accidently broke the handle of her coffee cup. Lukewarm Sanka spilled all over the floor and we had to clean it up. She swept up the broken pieces and threw them into her trash. I mopped. Afterwards we went for a walk.

Looking backwards into the minds of Oklahoma's top thinkers in the mid-sixties, I see that Mr. Bill was telling what he'd been taught in college. He didn't go into any details, of course, because we were in the sixth grade. Yet the question remains, why did I even consider what I'd been taught about American Indian ancestry? Perhaps I didn't fully realize the mischief of the colonizer's muse. She could make a Cherokee woman break her Japanese china in solidarity with the very nation-state that had stolen her homelands. Or tell stories to Native six-graders that our origins are elsewhere, not in America. A few months after I returned from Japan, I looked up the history of how American Indians became Mongols. Here's what I discovered. George Cuvier, a nineteenth-century French naturalist and zoologist, first applied the term "Mongolian" to American Indians as a racial classification. The Mongolian nomenclature stuck to us like glue. Later, English biologist Thomas Huxley applied Mongol to not only American Indians but also Arctic Natives. In 1940, anthropologist Franz Boaz included all Indigenous peoples of the Americas as part of the Mongoloid race. So drunk was Boaz on wistfulness that he scooped up the Aztec and Maya and stirred them into his bowl of Mongolian alphabet soup. Maybe that's why the US government forced American Indians onto reservations—to suppress the Mongols. I know, *I know*, a ridiculous idea. But after Pearl Harbor was attacked on December 7, 1941, Japanese Americans were sent to internment camps on or near Indian reservations. Meanwhile anthropologists still insist that Indigenous peoples of the Americas came from Asia. For Natives the most important story is yet to emerge, our memories of how we are related.

The Military Among Us

On that first evening when I rolled off the plane at Narita International, I noticed that all the flight information signs, airline names, and flight numbers were in English, which led me to believe that English was Japan's second language. Mitzuhito Kanehara was waiting for me at baggage claim outside of customs. We made the customary greetings and I bowed as I'd been taught in Iowa City.

"What would you like me to call you?" I asked.

"Kanehara. We are called by our last names."

"Call me LeAnne, please."

"Most kind. But most Japanese will prefer Miss Howe."

In the days that followed, I would find calling my host by his last name difficult and would occasionally slip, running *MmmKanehara* into one word. I'd become acquainted with him through our correspondence which he'd always signed "Mitzuhito Kanehara" or "M. Kanehara." So while in Japan I wrote "M. Kanehara" in my journal. Even now *MmmKanehara* seems right in this story.

Outside the airport we loaded my oversized bag in his car and headed toward the hotel in Shinjuku District. Along the way I noticed that all the highway signs were in Japanese and English. Again I assumed everyone spoke English or read English, that is, until I received the packet of information M. Kanehara gave me from the organizers of the International Forum on Anti-Discrimination and Human Rights. The program was entirely in Japanese and I couldn't make heads or tails of it. Days later when he translated it for me, my instructions were in "Military-ese."

10:22 begin speech.

Finish 12:13. Walk from the microphone. Kawasaki San will escort.

Meet conference officials 12:17.

18:00 finish work.

Follow escort to designated site for gathering.

Meal to commence at 18:19.

The precision of the schedule was another challenge, a difference I was afraid of. Could I end a speech at exactly 12:13 P.M. sharp? Since the forum was days away, I'd been booked into a hotel in the entertainment district, where I could wander around on my own and practice time management. Two minutes at each shop. Ten minutes at a glitzy bar. In the hotel room, I would turn over in bed, throw off the covers and step down into the bathroom cubicle—all in one move. A time-saver. The width of the double bed and the hotel room were the same. It had a western flush toilet, another time-saver, but I wouldn't realize how valuable it was until much later in my travels. Once I made the mistake of turning on the television in my room. A time-waster. A young Japanese girl, presumably naked, was cocooned entirely in cellophane wrap just like a larva before metamorphosis. Only her head was showing. She was hanging upside down by a set of heavy silver chains. An old Japanese man dressed in a gray business suit at least 69 or 70 years old was sticking needles into her skin. I wondered if he was playing the role of a spider. When the camera panned her body all the way down to the floor, the television audience could see that the girl was indeed crying out in ecstasy, not hideous pain. (No, I'm not kidding, and it wasn't a program about acupuncture.) I admit I was spellbound. After a while I turned the program off; I'd wasted ten minutes.

The Shinjuku District was rumored to be the inspiration for the 1982 sci-fi film *Blade Runner*. Maybe it was the huge TV screen on a building outside the train station. Or Shinjuku's narrow streets, exaggerated neon signs, skyscrapers, and beautiful Japanese metrosexuals, the essence of an otherworldly megalopolis that had captured the filmmaker's imagination.

The following excerpt is from my journal notes:

February 18, 1993: 2ⁿᵈ Night:

A big and bad Blade Runner *theme park.*

In Shinjuku no one sleeps

I discover comic book heaven for comic book lovers at 7-Eleven's Point-of-purchase rack. The fine quality of the bestiality depicted astounds me. Graphics of women and dogs, graphics of women and wild burros, graphics of female Superheroes intertwined with alligators. I know that particular sex act is hard to imagine but try. The mathematical combinations are staggering.

Crimony, why didn't I buy one when no one was looking?!

I'm told even Rupert Murdoch can be seen here on occasion

A glitzy karaoke lounge with emerging young talents in heels, both men and women

Two story color-changing neon signs that rotate into all sorts of new shapes.

Another bar that glows on contact
This is my kind of place!

On February 19, M. Kanehara and I traveled by train to visit Shinto shrines and later a famous Buddhist shrine in Kanagawa Prefecture. He'd taken a few days off from his university work to show me around Japan. We talked. His academic specialty was ethno-literature translation and he said he was interested in Native fiction writers. It was through his mother's connections with the Buraku Liberation League that he was able to invite me. He told me that discriminatory practices against the Buraku people in Japan have a long and complicated history, much like prejudices against American Indians in the United States. Discrimination against Buraku people has nothing to do with race, language, customs, or religions. Burakumin are wholly Japanese, unlike the Ainu, who are the indigenous people of Japan, or the Koreans of Japan that were brought in as forced laborers from 1939-1945.

Buraku history can be traced back to the feudalism of the Tokugawa Shogunate starting in the sixteenth century. Under Shogunate rule, people were put into four classes according to their occupations: samurai, farmers, artisans, and merchants. These classes were assumed to be a natural order of descending importance. Below the four classes were other groups of people known as outcastes, or untouchables, with occupations thought to be polluting, demanding, or undesirable. The untouchables were butchers, leather craftsman, entertainers, and flower arrangers. Artists.

"It's hard to understand isn't it?" I said. "Buraku people are the same as mainstream Japanese in all ways, but they're treated differently, like a racial minority in the US."

"Yes," he answered. "The Burakumin are members of a socially constructed minority. But isn't that the story in all societies?"

"How does one know if they're about to marry a Buraku person or mainstream Japanese?"

"The genealogy records of families go back centuries. Mothers and grandmothers can have the research done to make sure their daughters or granddaughters are not marrying into a Buraku family," he said.

"It's not exactly an analogy, but the Curtis Act in 1898 forced the Five Civilized Tribes to turn over their authority to determine tribal membership to the US Dawes Commission. Indians were enrolled by a blood quantum formula and families were tracked and catalogued. With each consecutive generation the blood quantum of tribal members would dwindle, especially since southeastern tribes were exogamous. In essence we were breeding ourselves out of existence. And White husbands of Native women could gain access to their wives' allotment lands."

"All roads lead to social constructions," he said. "With differing outcomes. Today Article 14 of the Constitution of Japan declares that all of the people are equal under the law and there can be no discrimination in political, economic, or social relations because of race, creed, sex, social status or family origin. But constructing identities will always be with us."

M. Kanehara said my lecture should discuss the challenges American Indians face at the end of the twentieth century in the United States. I assured him it would.

We then headed to The Great Buddha of Kamakura in Kanagawa Prefecture. It was bright and sunny at the site and felt so much warmer than Tokyo. Throughout the rest of the day we talked about various nuances in the works of American Indian writers. I'd brought gifts for my Japanese hosts: books by N. Scott Momaday, Leslie Marmon Silko, Paula Gunn Allen, Linda Hogan, Louise Erdrich, and Vine Deloria, Jr. He told me the names of some American writers that had been translated into Japanese as "Native."

"Jamake Highwater is not an American Indian," I said bluntly.

M. Kanehara appeared pensive.

"Highwater lied about his identity so much that eventually

the Smithsonian investigated his claims."

I explained that Jamake Highwater had a colorful but contradictory personal story. He first said he was born in Los Angeles, then Canada. "In high school he was called Jack or Jay Marks. He graduated in 1950 from Hollywood California High School; then it was reported in *Who's Who In America* that he was born in 1942, meaning he would have been seven when he graduated. He said he was of French-Canadian descent, then Blackfeet. He applied for all kinds of American Indian scholarships and received them."

M. Kanehara was thoughtful and didn't respond.

"This is fraud," I said angrily.

As we sat in front of the 13.35 meter-high bronze statue of the Buddha, I couldn't stop talking about ethnic frauds and how they were the modern equivalent of nineteenth-century Indian agents. In light of all the problems facing the world's indigenous peoples, I knew the fraudulent identity issue sounded trivial, but I wouldn't let it go.

"Indian agents once wielded great power over tribal peoples by usurping our traditional beliefs and eroding our traditional social roles. Today's ethnic frauds do the same things. They invent beliefs and practices that never existed and then publish a book of lies. Unfortunately most scholars are duped into teaching the works of ethnic frauds." I yammered on and on like some kind of manic. I don't excuse my irreverence at the temple site except to say I wasn't seeing the statue of Buddha. Nor was I seeing the other tourists there. I was seeing Choctaw people in the Lower Mississippi Valley in 1738. Smallpox blankets arrived in the east and were traded west, along with the smell of oblivion—gifts from hairy-fingered foreigners. I was seeing our warriors fall and get up, fall and get up, then walk through a door that centuries later I would emerge from, my fists clenched at birth, screaming who wants to fight? I was seeing myself, a warrior engaged in a desperate battle I will not win, enemies on all sides. Then suddenly I awakened in the sunlight, surrounded by lush greenery and hackberry trees, frightened by the raging woman I'd become at the Buddhist shrine.

"While our tribes are fighting the government in federal court, these ethnic frauds market themselves as medicine men, charging hundreds of dollars to unwitting people who want an exotic 'Indian' ceremony."

M. Kanehara was solemn now, withdrawn. I'd bullied him into silence. When he finally spoke I measured the distance of the words between what he said and what he thought. I liked M. Kanehara, yet I'd shown myself a fool. I'd wounded him, a man gracious enough to bring me to Japan. I dug in my purse for a tissue to wipe my eyes and pulled out my journal. *Something to write on. Some way to mark my shame.* Suddenly a band of Japanese Baptist Missionaries swept by us, fervently praising God as they passed around a collection plate at The Great Buddha of Kamakura.

"Just as we're about to lose our bearings, fate lends a hand," he said serenely.

I looked up from my journal and tried to smile.

M. Kanehara stood up. His face tranquil, eyes judicious, regretting me, I supposed, and yet he was deferential. He said that we should circle the large stationary object that may or may not have known it was being watched. After we circled the Buddha, I walked alone for a time outside the sanctuary, thinking about the images I'd just conjured up.

Memories. Whose are they? Is the pain I carry mine, or my family's? Does it come through blood ties, stories, or both? If so, we're all carriers. Facing toward the Buddha I silently asked again, "Whose memories?" Then listened to the weight of knowing.

Loy E. Billy died in WWII, shot to pieces two weeks after his nineteenth birthday. My uncle. Just a boy, really, only five foot three inches tall, 124 pounds. At sixteen, Loy enlisted in September of 1940 on the same day as his older brother Schlicht Billy, who was three months shy of his twentieth birthday. Loy lied on his enlistment application saying he was nineteen. Both my uncles listed "actor" as their civil occupations. Apparently no one in the enlistment office could read irony. Uncle Loy was a fighter. I have pictures of him in boxing gloves, dukes up. He fought in amateur boxing matches in McAlester and wanted to become a Golden Gloves champion. Because he'd only finished grammar school, he became a private, eventually serving in the Army's Company "F," 180th Infantry Regiment, 45th Infantry Division.

Uncle Schlicht was a Second Lieutenant in command of Fox Company and Loy's commanding officer. Over the course of Schlicht's service he was wounded four times and received a Purple Heart, a Good Conduct Medal, an American Defense Service Ribbon, a European African Medal with a cluster of five Bronze Stars, and two Silver Stars. He was also a Choctaw Code Talker in WWII. In 2008, Schlicht was awarded a Congressional Gold Medal, posthumously, along with all the other Choctaw Code Talkers of WWI and WWII. But Schlicht's greatest act of heroism might have been pulling his brother up off the ground the day Loy was killed. Together they took a step forward into hope, and then acceptance. A specimen of ruin. The pure light that took Uncle's place that day still remembers him, as does his family. Carrying the memory of it is hard. Without warning, it can cut through flesh and bone, revealing its truest nature—a crushed diamond.

Later that evening, after M. Kanehara dropped me at my hotel, I searched in my purse for another tissue and found a small pamphlet titled, "The Great Buddha of Kamakura." I'd forgotten I had it. One of the lines jumped out at me. "The central teaching is that through devotion to Amida Buddha, expressed through mantras and sincerity of the heart, one will go to the Pure Land, or 'Western Paradise' after death—a pleasant realm from which it is easy to attain nirvana."

"*Itadakimasu*," I said quietly as a prayer, both hands on my heart. "I humbly receive."

Memories Without Fixed Finality

February 22, 1993: Day 6

Things I have seen, been told, learned.

Japanese people wear masks when they have colds so as not to infect others.

Very sensible. Americans should adopt this custom.

Mount Fuji is an Ainu name. Each May the landscape is pink with moss.

Many place names in Japan are Ainu, the indigenous people of Hokkaido.

No one I've met in Japan speaks English save M. Kanehara. And one of his students.

The bank currency exchange officer in Tokyo doesn't speak English.

She pointed and gestured, but has no English.

So far I can say three words in Japanese. Ohayo gozaimasu. Good morning.

But I said it to the hotel clerk as I was leaving for dinner. Wrong again.

February 23, 1993: Day 7

I attend Kabuki-Za, Tokyo's premier kabuki theater in Ginza.

First show opened in 1889. The location may have been the residence of the Hosokawa, a Japanese samurai clan descended from Emperor Seiwa (850-880).

If a French voyageur in the 18th century had written

about a Choctaw storytelling performance

he might have written something like this,

"1718 at the Chickasawhay Village,

home of the Imoklasha, the war clan.

Storytelling continues three days now. More to come.

Merde!"

In Japan

Kabuki is a five hour-long theater production.

(I think I might have been brought here to give my handlers a rest.)

Rich Japanese women come to kabuki dressed in kimonos, white socks, thongs, and mink stoles.

They carry small wooden Bento boxes into Kabuki-Za.

Bento boxes are filled with Japanese delicacies

to be eaten during intermission.

My box was filled with Sushi and beer.

Very sensible.

Sama, gives praise to the one who makes the meal.

First Hour.

Mystified. First play written in 1751. Scenery bright. All men.

To add perspective, as if we're watching a scene happening far away,

children replace male actors onstage. Adorable.

Three Hours Pass.

Second play.

Story about a ghost, a female courtesan, I think.

Spit out beer, I wasn't expecting everyone to die.

Hour Four.

A droning eternity.

Third play, all swords, no blood.

Considered modern when it was written in 1883.

Fifth Hour:

I commit Hara-kiri.

February 24, 1993: Day 8
More new sights.
Tokyo Bay, and the Monorail.
Then a jet to Okayama Prefecture
We meet a group of men at the Buraku Liberation League
The headquarters in Okayama City is impressive.
M. Kanehara returns to Tokyo
to give exams to his university students.
I miss him.
My homestay family does not speak English
Why didn't I learn at least some Japanese?
Damn it.

All Roads Lead to Social Constructions

My homestay family brought me back to the Buraku Liberation League headquarters the next morning. The translator arrived as well. Matsuo San, a translator by profession, had been assigned to render my twenty-five-page speech into something coherent for the audience at the International Forum on Anti-Discrimination and Human Rights. I knew he had his work cut out for him. "We will improvise, *LeAnnehowe San*, do not to worry."

"You don't seem entirely convinced of that," I said smiling.

"It will happen as it should."

Matsuo San was tall and very thin. He spoke English perfectly. Because it was still so very cold he was dressed in a sweater vest and long sleeve shirt, a coat and tie. He was also a Japanese human rights activist, passionate about ending the Indonesian occupation of East Timor and the military's abuses against women there. He and others had been demonstrating in Osaka and other cities to raise awareness about the plight of East Timor. Matsuo San had once lived in California while working towards his university degree in translation studies. He was married to Masako, but as of yet they had no children.

I was delighted to be working with him. Matsuo San was an extrovert and someone with whom I could practice some new Japanese words. Within an hour he corrected my bowing. "Bend head, body forward, but do not press your hands so tightly against your body as if glued there." That was progress. For the next few hours Matsuo San and I went over the lecture. He wrote a list of my words and specific phrasings in his journal. I couldn't help but notice it was similar to the one I carried. "They help me translate your meaning correctly," he said.

Later that evening we went for our "first rehearsal," a short speaking engagement before a group of public school teachers. We performed very well together. I slowed my speaking voice and killed all idiomatic Oklahoma phrases such as "I'm fixin' to" and "a blind hog finds an acorn once in a while." Matsuo San said my English was easy to understand and I took this as a compliment to my home training.

The Japanese teachers talked about world history. They'd read some American Indian history, but still didn't know that tribes squared off against the US government on disputes over treaty rights, hunting and fishing rights, or water and mineral rights. I also spoke about the subtleties of race in America. I told the story of how a female tax accountant in Iowa City, Iowa, once pointed at me in a public meeting and shouted, "You people don't even pay taxes!"

I shot back, "No, Madam, we laugh all the way to the bank." Matsuo San had to explain several times why my retort was supposed to be funny before the Japanese teachers laughed. After that I stayed away from irony.

Day eleven. On my second night in Okayama Prefecture, I would stay in the home of Kawasaki San, a man who was truly a credit to strong-willed union bosses everywhere. In public he was self-absorbed, intolerant of interruptions, a man used to giving orders. At the Buraku Liberation League headquarters Kawasaki San seemed the embodiment of three men: John L. Lewis, formidable leader of the United Mine Workers of America; Samuel Gompers, longest-serving president of the American Federation of Labor (AFL); and Teamster Boss Jimmy Hoffa. He seemed unafraid to confront corporate powers or the Japanese government, and, most important, Kawasaki San was the boss of me. To this day, I'm not sure what his role was in organizing the 1993 United Nations International Year of the World's Indigenous People, but he must have been in charge of the international guests. He also seemed to be working for the Buraku Liberation League, yet he and his family were not Burakumin. (I asked.)

Once we arrived at his home, Kawasaki San was kind and accommodating. The entire family was a joy to be with, although they didn't speak English; and though I was losing my fear of trying to speak Japanese, every word I spoke was unintelligible. But considering we had no words, we communicated very well. Mrs. Kawasaki's hobby was growing flowers of all kinds. She and I stayed up late looking through her flower magazines. We were almost the same age, although I'm a month older. They had three teenage children, and she and her husband had been married twenty years.

At this time of year all the homes were iceboxes. Frost on the windows. No indoor heat except space heaters. I wore my red warrior coat to bed and wrapped a shawl around my head to try and keep warm. The toilets were Western. *No furry heated seats*; yet there was a small water heater in the bathroom that played the *William Tell Overture*, theme music for the *Lone Ranger and Tonto* television show, as the water heated for washing hands. I pondered whether they'd programmed the music to make me feel at home or ill at ease.

How Many Next Times Will There Be?

In 1993 it was estimated that there were 300 million
Indigenous people living in seventy countries. The Natives of
the Americas, the Inuit and Aleutians of the circumpolar region,
the Aborigines and Torres Strait Islanders of Australia and
the Maori of New Zealand, along with the Saami of northern
Europe, are all Indigenous peoples. Quoting from a United
Nations report, "more than 60 percent of Bolivia's population is
indigenous, and Indigenous peoples make up roughly half the
populations of Guatemala and Peru. China and India together
have more than 150 million indigenous and tribal people. Some
ten million indigenous people live in Myanmar."

Much of the world's foods, such as potatoes, corn, beans,
squash, tomatoes, peanuts, sugar cane, pumpkins, peppers, and
cocoa, which is chocolate, were first cultivated in the Americas
by Native agriculturalists. According to the UN report, it was
estimated that seventy-five percent of the world's plant-based
pharmaceuticals, including aspirin, quinine, and digitalis, were
derived from medicinal plants first used by Indigenous peoples.

On the day of the International Human Rights Forum,
the air was electric. Some 800 people attended. TV cameras,
newspaper reporters, and Japanese dignitaries were also there. I
was told we made the evening news on the Japanese CBS-equiv-
alent, and was given copies of the three newspapers that covered
the event, all in Japanese, but I was grateful to have them.

For the first time in my life, four Indigenous people were
telling our stories to an audience that just might carry them as we
have carried them. I wondered how many next times will there be
like this? Maybe none? My only regret was that M. Kanehara was
not able to attend as I'd hoped. I wanted to redeem myself in his
eyes through a more measured lecture about American Indians.

The other three speakers were Mr. Eeda, Ainu, from
Hokkaido; Alan Brown, Koorie, Aborigine from Australia; and
Illia Janovich, Sinti Roma from Austria. I was the first to speak
for eighty minutes. Matsuo San's translations were heroic. For

the first six pages we followed my text earnestly; then I started to improvise. He had his book of keywords that he'd written, and together we wove a story of what it meant to be Indigenous in the United States five hundred and one years after first contact with Europeans.

I told a modern story about a proposal for a hazardous waste site that Choctaw Chief Phillip Martin of the Mississippi Band of Choctaw Indians had agreed to build in Noxubee County, Mississippi, part of the original homelands of our tribe. The project was straightforward. A company would build a hazardous waste dumpsite, and Choctaws would be the keepers of this waste. This inflamed many members of the Mississippi Band of Choctaw Indians, that they should do all the dirty work for an outside corporation. They organized protests alongside their non-Indian neighbors against Chief Philip Martin. The hazardous waste dumpsite project was defeated in a tribal vote and Martin had to return the "earnest" money.

"We are not our brothers' keepers," I said ending my lecture. Matsuo San's translations, my words, our lecture.

Mr. Eeda spoke next about the Ainu. He was dressed in traditional Ainu regalia, with a thin band tied around his head. He said (through a translator) that during the Meji period the Ainu were known as savages. In 1924 the Ainu were accepted as Japanese, the same year that most American Indians were given the right to vote in America. The Hokkaido Ainu Association was formed in 1930. The Manchurian Incident (the Japanese term for the beginning of WWII) halted any progress for the Ainu. They reorganized again in 1953. Mr. Eeda noted another similarity to Native Americans: the Ainu were currently fighting the Japanese government in the courts for placing hazardous waste dumps on their lands.

Alan Brown, Koorie, an Aboriginal tribe in Australia, spoke next. His aunt founded the Aboriginal Health Services in his region. Unlike the Indian Health Service clinics run by Uncle Sam in the US, the Aboriginal people own, operate, and hire all medical personnel that work in their clinics. Brown said the government and anthropologists tell Aboriginal peoples that they've only been in Australia for 40,000 years. "The question we ask is," said Brown, "why this isn't long enough to establish indigenous residency." He also said Aboriginal tribes have been wracked by disease and explained that the English instigated the first germ warfare by smearing the smallpox virus on blankets they traded to the Aborigines.

I immediately thought of Lord Jeffery Amherst; how he had allowed the trading of smallpox blankets to the American Indians in 1763. Smallpox wiped out whole tribes. Amherst, Massachusetts, was named after Lord Jeffery, and later Amherst College was named for the town. (Genocide pays.)

Illia Janovich spoke about the issues the Sinti Roma faced in Austria. He spoke of their history and the forced deportation of the Sinti and the Roma from Asperg, Germany in May 22, 1940. And still discrimination against Sinti Roma people, formerly known as gypsies, continued. Janovich's organization was currently struggling to ensure that Sinti Roma children could receive an education. By the end of his talk, everyone in the audience was teary-eyed. Perhaps it was the power of all our stories that made them cry. We made ourselves cry. Indigenous peoples are still struggling to survive; that's the story. Will this audience that is engaged in protecting human rights carry our stories across nations? Will they remember as we remember? Will I carry the stories of Hiroshima, Nagasaki? Hokkaido? Asperg? Is this how we make the human family? Through stories? I long to know.

After an exhausting ten-hour day, Alan Brown, Mr. Eeda, Illia Janovich and I still wanted to spend some quiet time together. But we were told there was no time due to our tight schedules. Each of us was scheduled to lecture in different towns the next morning. We were herded into separate vehicles heading in opposite directions. Then suddenly Mr. Eeda turned away from his handlers and raced toward the car I was in. As the driver started the engine, Mr. Eeda put his hands on the back windshield; he was crying. I quickly put my palms against the glass to show that I was feeling what he was feeling. Mr. Eeda ran a few steps alongside the car and I wanted to get out and run with him, but the car sped off. I can still see him standing in the road watching us drive away. In solidarity, we understood there would never be a next time. Only the stories.

More Memories Without Fixed Finality

March, something? 1993?

I've been here two and a half weeks, longer, I think.

I'm a blur moving through space

Feel like a prisoner.

More meetings.

New people, hour after hour.

Mayors and government officials, too.

Everywhere I go they give me beautiful bouquets of flowers.

Gifts.

I say stupid things like

Oh, marvelous

What sublimity!

Truly a vision

WTF

Yesterday, at an ESL school,

I pose for 25 individual pictures with each child in the school.

They are all so beautiful.

The mother of the son that owns the ESL school says to me,

(in the public meeting where I'm lecturing)

"I spent a lot of money on my son's education
so he can teach English and this Indian
speaks better than him."
Matsuo San was embarrassed to translate.

Tonight I stay in a farmhouse.
An indoor outhouse toilet.
They do not have hot water tanks,
but the family owns four brand-new automobiles.
(Like some Indians I know)
Fugimoro's house.
Itadakimasu: I humbly receive.

Last Toilet Fiasco

What I remember is this. The Fugimoros were Burakumin and very nervous. I was doing a homestay with them and was very tired. Before the meal, they escorted me to their indoor-outhouse. I took off the house shoes they'd given me to wear inside the home, and they directed me to put on another pair of shoes to enter the indoor-outhouse. With much trepidation I went in alone.

There was a hole in the floor with a small white porcelain bowl turned upside down at one end. No handles. I had been drinking lots of green tea—again. I struggled to remove my clothes and figure out what to do. I tried to sit on the smooth, cold porcelain surface. I stood up. I angled over the hole and crouched backwards as if I was a limbo dancer from Trinidad. "I'm dying here," I said aloud. Finally I put my clothes back on, walked outside, and changed back into the first pair of house shoes and walked into the room where Matsuo San and Kawasaki San were visiting with the Fugimoros.

"I need your help," I said bluntly. "I can't figure out the proper use of their toilet."

Matsuo San translated. Everyone in the room was embarrassed but me. (I was holding it in.) I could feel the eyes of the family asking what kind of imbecile they'd invited to stay in their home. The whole family walked me back to the indoor outhouse. They changed their shoes, I changed my shoes, Matsuo San changed his shoes, and we all gathered around the hole in the floor as he showed me how to utilize the porcelain bowl "like a woman." (That's right. Number one *and* number two.)

"LeAnnehowe San, we must make draw instructions for foreigners that show them how to use our toilets."

I bowed and agreed. Another incorrect gesture when one is in the indoor-outhouse, but by this time I was desperate for them to leave. Alone at last in the room, I peed.

Yet, the night was young and things only went downhill from there. The Fugimoro family had invited the mayor and other local dignitaries to dine with them and their guests from the International Human Rights' Forum. After the toilet training incident, I'd had enough of crowds and needed some downtime. During the meal I leaned over to Matsuo San and asked if I could go to a hotel for the next night and have a day's rest. "No lectures." I naively thought that we would have a conversation about it after dinner and decide how to proceed. But that was not to be. Just after the fish soup had been served Matsuo San translated my request aloud in front of the entire Fugimoro family, the mayor, the other guests, and Kawasaki San.

Mr. Fugimoro reacted immediately by throwing his chopsticks across the *chabudai*, a low flat table for hosting guests. He shouted something in Japanese, then in English. "No, no, no," he cried. (For real, he was crying.) Oh god, I had brought shame on the Fugimoro house. Mrs. Fugimoro did not cry but eyeballed me with a look that said, "You indigenous bitch!" I read her loud and clear.

"I don't want to leave your lovely home," I said in English. "I only wanted to go to a hotel tomorrow night. This has nothing to do with your gracious hospitality. I'm sorry." By now Matsuo San was standing. Near spitting out his words, I reasoned that he was trying to set things right. Kawasaki San had jumped up off the floor and adjusted the belt to his slacks before he began speaking. (I'd forgotten I was traveling with Japan's Jimmy Hoffa.) Once Kawasaki San spoke, everyone stopped talking and listened. He would be the one to save face for Mr. Fugimoro. He would be the one to save face for me. I sat there listening to words I couldn't understand, wishing I was dead.

Arrangements were settled. Matsuo San and I would spend the night with the Fugimoro family even after the unfortunate incident over dinner. No more talking.

Breakfast the next morning was difficult. I was awakened at 5 A.M. and served a bowl of lukewarm fish head soup. I drank it down and thanked Mrs. Fugimoro profusely. She barely acknowledged my presence. Mr. Fugimoro's face was still swollen from being so distraught. There were no ceremonial good-byes. No one bowed.

This Is the Story I Didn't Want to Tell

Just when I thought I couldn't make things worse, I did. The next day we traveled to another small town in the countryside where we met with more Japanese teachers and school children. One of the men at the school, Mr. Akihito (not his real name), was a Japanese soldier in WWII, which, as noted earlier, began with the "Manchurian Incident." We had tea with him and his family because he told Matsuo San that he wanted to ask me some questions. He'd been a Japanese prisoner of war, captured by the Americans. He still had mixed feelings about Americans, he said. What he wanted to know was if there was still a lot of prejudice against Japanese people. "Jap, Jap," he said in English. Matsuo San said Mr. Akihito wanted to know if Americans still used this derogatory term. I paused and thought long before answering. Now, I'd heard this term all my life growing up in Oklahoma. I also heard it on the trading desk at my former securities firm. But to Mr. Akihito, I decided to tell a different story.

"I once worked for a Wall Street securities firm," I said. "The manager in New York told me he'd married a JAP. I must have looked confused because he laughed and said that his wife was a Jewish American Princess, a JAP."

"He was joking on an acronym," I said. "No one uses the word 'Jap' for Japanese any longer."

Matsuo San knew I was lying. Mr. Akihito knew I was lying, his family knew I was lying. But I just couldn't go through another emotional scene like the night before. So I lied and the lie remains buried inside me, unjustified, untenable, a shame that I must always carry.

The journey home, as I remembered it, was overwhelming. When we returned to Osaka, it was Kawasaki San who escorted me to the train that would take me back to Tokyo. As I stepped inside the train the glass door closed quickly. My friend put his hand up to the glass, just as Mr. Eeda had many days before. I raised my hand. We didn't drop our eyes as the train quickly pulled away. We knew there would never be a next time.

What I wrote in my journal just before the plane took off from Narita International for the US was this:

Fog thickens and thins all
the days I've been in Japan.
Green, green, I've never seen such
vibrant emerald mountains and fields,
set against a titan blue sky.
Magnificent, even in winter.
Yakne achukma, good land in Choctaw.

If our bodies are an epic landscape that carries the stories of human existence, of our ancestors, of ourselves, of memories without fixed finality, perhaps someday American Indians will remember how we're related to the Japanese. Maybe. I know I yearn to be forgiven for the disrespect I showed to The Great Buddha of Kamakura and my friend M. Kanehara, for my many other cross-cultural mistakes, most especially with all manner of toilets and washing apparatuses.

Japan. *Honno o shirushi de gozai masu ga.* It only amounts to a symbol of my appreciation.

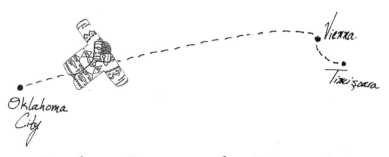

Oklahoma City

Vienna

Timișoara

Carlos Castaneda Lives in Romania

One spring afternoon in 1998, a fierce gust of floral winds blew me, and my Toyota RAV4, off I-80 near Iowa City, Iowa. It was April 27; I remember it precisely because I'd just taught a unit on American Indians to my Monday class at Grinnell College. I'd used an eighteenth-century Choctaw warrior named Red Shoes as an example of a charismatic leader who eventually turned on his own people. Hours later I ended up in a ditch near a stand of trees. Rather than explain to the wrecker driver that a strange wind pushed me into the ditch (it was a cloudless perfect day), I said a deer ran across the road. This happened so frequently in Iowa that he took my word for it. But it was the wind. As I've been told many times, cosmic forces such as a violent invisible wind often announce great change. I thought perhaps I was going to finally lose some weight, but that would come much later and without warning

The next day I received an invitation from the Center for Complexity Studies in Reșița, Romania to attend a ten-day summer seminar. Our panel titled "Cultural Communications and Understanding of Otherness" was about fostering pro-active attitudes towards protecting nature, the biosphere, and cultural diversity. Invited scholars and artists would stay at Raul Alb, White River Leisure Camp, from August 4-14, 1998. We would give lectures that supported the theme. While the Romanian-English translation was a bit stilted, I re-translated the invitation this way: The seminar organizers were beginning a Romanian environmental movement and they needed an American Indian along with others from the biosphere to help. I looked up tourist sites on the map and found that Bran Castle, commonly known as Dracula's castle, was only 248 miles away from Reșița. (Possible road trip.) I replied at once to the invitation and said my lectures would be themed around "Spaces and the Production of the Sacred" and subsequently arranged it with them for Jim Wilson, my husband, to attend and lecture on "Family Politics, Family Place." (Poor man. He has oodles of experiential research to draw from. "Married into a large Choctaw family" should be a separate line on his CV.)

Before setting off for the land of Dacia, Jim and I returned home to Ada, Oklahoma, prepared our lectures, gathered materials for the seminar, and bought indigenous gifts.

What follows is more or less what happened.

We fly from New York to Vienna, Austria, where we have a six-hour layover before traveling on to our final destination, Reșița, Romania. At Wien (pronounced Vine), we rock and roll out of the airport in search of the Demel Shop on Kolhmarkt, Vienna's most famous confectioner. If you haven't been to the Demel Shop and ordered a classic chocolate Sachertorte, try to imagine a layer of scrumptious, mouth-watering milk chocolate frosting covering a simple cake but with a layer of apricot jam just beneath the icing. (Academic fieldwork is rough.)

Yet, I have to say, the chocolatier in Vienna has a way to go to compete with Ada Oklahoma's sensational chocolatier Edna Sixkiller (Cherokee). Sixkiller has been molding chocolates in four distinctive shapes and sizes since 1979, when her parents built Big Wings Truckstop, Ice Cream Parlor, and Package Store (henceforth Big Wings) off highway 3W in Ada. The sign above the cash register in Big Wings reads, "After 500 years it only seems right that American Indians are getting back in the chocolate business."

So in preparation for our journey, I'd loaded up on four dozen individually-wrapped chocolates in the shape of cowboy boots, cowboy hats, peanut-cluster cowpatties, and the ever-popular Pocahontas-on-a-stick. Gifts for the Romanians. (As a Native, it's imperative that I have easy access to authentic indigenous foods.)

Chocolate, the so-called food of the gods, comes from the cocoa tree and is indigenous to the New World. According to archaeologists, cacao or cocoa beans were cultivated in Central America as early as 1500 BCE. Yet, tourists around the world believe chocolate is *Old World*, originating in Switzerland, Germany, France, Italy, or Austria. Research into the history of Conquistador Hernán Cortés de Monroy y Pizarro, truly a first-rate crime boss of his era, reveals that whenever he forced Aztec ruler Moctezuma II to dine with him in 1519, they drank a local concoction, hot chocolate mixed with vanilla derived from a most delicate orchid. Buckets of it.

Back to Demel in Vienna.

We seat ourselves at a small table on the second floor. In order to expense the taxi rides and pricey Sachertortes at Demel, I'll have to ask a few questions of the waitstaff as part of my research on the proliferation of chocolate worldwide, circa 1500 to the present.

"Can I get a glass of water with my espresso?"

"Mineral or sparkling?" asks the waiter.

"Sparkling, thanks. When did Demel open?"

"It's complicated. Read the brochure," he says, writing on a pad.

"Who was the confectioner that integrated chocolate and cake flour?"

"No idea, read the brochure." He pauses. "American, right?"

"It's complicated. American Indian, I'm Choctaw?"

He looks from his receipt book to us. "Remarkable, I was just reading *The Teachings of Don Juan* by Carlos Castaneda. Amazing shaman."

"Shaman is not the right…"

"Such spiritual powers," he continues. "Do all American Indian tribes have shamans such as don Juan?"

"Great question, Sigmund." (His nametag.)

"Call me Ziggy. Your tribe doesn't have shamans, no? So sad."

At this point Jim interrupts the fieldwork interview. "We're flying out later today to Reșița, Romania," he says. "Since we had a long layover in Vienna, we came straight to Demel for a shot of sugar and a dose of people watching. Can you bring us the bill when you serve the water?"

Ziggy departs quickly. I believe he'll rush right back for a healthy debate on don Juan, the shaman. But Demel is buzzing with international tourists.

Jim turns to me and whispers, "I had to say something or we'd have been here all day debating Carlos Castaneda and his books."

"Would not."

"Would too."

"Na-uh."

"Ya-hah."

Ziggy never returns but another waiter drops the bill on the table as if it were a used handkerchief. A half hour later, we leave the famous Austrian chocolatier and hail a taxi. Jim asks the driver to take us back to the airport the long way. "Can you drive us around Wien for an hour or so and point out the sights."

"Mnaa," he says. "Yes."

A Greek cabbie. When Thanos (name on the taxi license) realizes Jim once lived in Athens and speaks Greek, they talk like long-lost friends, finishing each other's sentences.

"You were there?"

"Me also."

"Remarkable isn't it?"

When they switch into Greek, the taxi swerves on and off the Viennese pavements making me dizzy.

"He's reviving my Greek soul," Jim says, laughing.

"I revive also," says Thanos. They continue chatting gleefully as we drive around Vienna. Occasionally Thanos remembers to point out major landmarks.

"There, Hofburg Palace. Very famous," says Thanos.

I look out the window at the palace that was once the home of the Habsburg, dynasty rulers of the Austro-Hungarian Empire. My companions continue in what can only be described as Greco-English. I catch the name Melina Mercouri, the sexiest woman in Greece's Golden Age of Cinema. Jim says, "Grigoris Lambrakis," and I guess he's referring to the Lambrakis's assassination in 1963. A famous Greek leftist, his life was the basis for the film *Z*.

"I know Santorini…" says Jim.

"The doors are…

"…the blue of the Aegean."

"Museumsquartier," says Thanos. "Very famous."

I read about it in the guidebook. Museums, nightlife, art galleries. From the back of the taxi I couldn't see much.

Now Jim and Thanos have shifted to the economy in Greece and its current inflation rate. The conversation goes into overdrive. Thanos' eyes narrow as he curses the heavens in Greek. He raises his hands in frustration, lets go of the wheel, and talks (evidently) to Athena, the goddess of wisdom, courage, civilization, mathematics, law, and justice. The taxicab, sensing that Thanos has temporarily lost his mind over Greece's escalating inflation, goes on autopilot and zigzags through the streets of Wien. I stifle a desperate squeal, preferring to trust the universe. Jim sits stock straight, looking toward trance. Somehow we arrive safely back at the airport. In the future I will explain the taxi ride as an imagined event, one that never happened, but could have happened, otherwise we wouldn't be alive and in one piece. Intoxicated drivers of all races report the same phenomenon, "The car drove itself, Your Honor; it wasn't me."

As we get out of the cab, we shake hands with Thanos and say fare-thee-well. I give him a chocolate cowboy boot from my bag, assuring him that Edna Sixkiller makes the best chocolate in the universe. He wishes us safe travels in Romania. "Yes, Dracula, I know him," he says, "the blood drinker. When you meet Dracula speak Greek to him. He hates Ottomans and all Turks. If he approach you, tell him what Socrates say. 'I know nothing except the fact of my ignorance.' He will not want to drink the blood of such an intelligent Greek."

The flight to Timişoara, Romania, isn't crowded. Our afternoon lunch consists of chicken cordon bleu, tender greens, and a side of baby carrots. Sekt, Austria's sparkling wine, is served in a cold champagne glass along with the meal. The flatware is Gorham wrapped in cloth napkins. Honestly, I think we've been catapulted back into the late 1960s when airlines like TWA and Braniff International Airways offered cloth napkins and silverware on most cross-country flights. These days you're lucky to get a cup of lukewarm water.

Soon another absolutely ravishing flight attendant appears, this one with light brown hair and vibrant blue eyes. (Swedish, I think.) "I would be pleased to pour you second glass of Sekt," she says.

I note her resemblance to the beautiful actress Ingrid Bergman. We hold up our glasses for refills.

"My yes," says Jim, "but let's not count them. After we land in Timişoara we're expected to attend a working seminar."

"Your secret is safe with me," she says smiling.

We arrive safely and on time at the gate. All thirty passengers deplane by air stairs. The sun is bright and it's a very warm day, August 3, 1998. Yet, everyone on our flight is dressed fit to kill. The women wear high heels, off-white business suits, and fedoras. It gives the impression that Romania has landed on its stilettos since the revolution in 1989. We won't know just how false our first impressions are until much later in the journey. We have no personal connections with Romania. What knowledge we have is purely historical, obtained by reading newspaper clippings, books, and maps.

As we walk the thirty yards or so toward the terminal entrance at Timişoara, there's a noticeable mood change. Something is in the air. Something I've not encountered before. I remind myself that I'm a foreigner and know so very little about Romania. This is no time to make judgments. But I take thirteen seconds to make a list of what I do know. There's Vlad the Impaler, so named because he impaled thousands of Muslims on large stakes in his front yard; Bela Lugosi (you know what he's famous for); Nicolae Ceauşescu, the communist party boss killed on Christmas for crimes against humanity; and Romanian writer Andrei Codrescu, a regular guest on NPR who wrote *The Blood Countess* and a jillion other books. I love his writing.

Shrugging off my uneasiness, I chalk it up to Sekt and too many Hollywood films starring Bela Lugosi. Before I step inside the building I see my shadow squirm in the sunlight, but go in anyway. Suddenly a fissure of music discords against the ever-popular Gipsy Kings playing on someone's boom box inside the building.

"Hey, that kinda sounds like a theme song from *Casablanca,*" says Jim. "I'm sure it's Max Steiner's Warner Brothers Studio Orchestra from the 1940s."

I nod in agreement. "Yeah, but it's a bad mashup. The Reyes brothers' vocals sound unnatural against Steiner's strings." Just as the words leave my lips, the timpani drums drown out the music and muffled thunder rolls beneath our every move. A subliminal signal used in classic Hollywood films that tells the audience when something unusual and unexpected is about to happen. We pick up our bags and carry them slowly toward

Checkpoint Charlie, the three customs officers waiting for us at a long gray table.

I know what you're thinking. Checkpoint Charlie is the name Western Allies gave the infamous crossing point between East and West Berlin during the Cold War. Why am I using the name "Checkpoint Charlie" in Romania? While we're not in Germany and the Cold War ended in 1989, this feels like a highly charged border crossing in which anything can happen. I dunno, I didn't write the script. I'm an actor. A chill runs through my body when I see that we're the last foreigners in line. The timpani drums still muffle softly on the sound system as we approach three plainclothesmen.

These colorless and nameless men look us over; then one unzips the tiny pockets of my carry-on. One male, whom I also dub "Checkpoint Charlie," pulls out an individually wrapped Pocahontas-on-a-stick. "She's all yours," I say. "A gift. Just dunk her in your morning coffee."

My bribe has little effect. It's clear we're going to be interrogated and I suspect them of being the unfortunate former employees of the Directorate for Counterespionage in Romania. I've read about them in *TIME* magazine. Once their job was to protect Romanians from foreigners like us, ideologues with books on poststructuralist theory. Now they're here to confuse unsuspecting tourists drunk on uh-hem, X number of glasses of Sekt.

I should explain one more detail. Before leaving for New York I received a suspicious email from a person who shall remain anonymous. I was told to say that we've come to Romania for tourism. Tourism, I thought, WTF?!

"Why have you come to Timişoara?" Charlie speaks English with a German accent. I'm not surprised. (According to the 1992 census I read in the library, 119,462 Germans live in Romania.)

"For tourism," I say.

"Tourism?"

"Yes, I've come to see the sights."

"What sights?"

"The churches, towns, the people." I casually pull a tube of lipstick out of my bag and reapply red to my lips. To my amazement, the lipstick turns into a Camel cigarette, filterless, and I take a puff and blow it into the face of Checkpoint Charlie.

"There's nothing to see in Timişoara. What is the purpose of your trip to Romania?"

"Tourism." Over the airport's loudspeakers the theme music from *Casablanca* drones on. (This is intolerable.)

Charlie presses for more information. He looks over his notes. Then right before my very eyes turns into Major Heinrich Strasser, the German bad guy played by Conrad Veidt in *Casablanca*. "Do you mind if I ask you a few questions? Unofficially, of course."

"Make it official if you like?" I say, blowing more smoke into the air.

"What is your nationality?"

"I'm a drunkard."

"That makes Choctaw Indians citizens of the world," says the other plainclothesman who now looks suspiciously like Captain Renault, played by Claude Rains. He tears the wrapper off the chocolate Pocahontas and licks her head.

"I was born in a home for unwed Indian women, in Edmond, Oklahoma, if that'll help you any. My birth mother didn't bother to check whether I was male or female. Just walked out on me pretending I never happened."

Major Strasser and Captain Renault exchange looks, but say nothing.

"I understand that you've come here from Wien."

"There seems to be no secret about that, it's stamped right on my passport."

"Are you one of those people who can't imagine the Germans in their beloved Timişoara?" asks Strasser.

"It's not particularly my beloved Timişoara."

"Can you imagine us in Choctaw Country?" says the fat balding plainclothesman.

Since he has no other lines in the script, just a nameless extra, I turn to him and snap, "When you get there, ask me!"

"How about Ada?" says Major Heinrich Strasser.

I look directly at Strasser. "Well, there are certain sections of Ada, Major, that I wouldn't advise you to try to invade. Big Wings, for starters. Southeastern Indians are very sensitive about Edna Sixkiller and her chocolates."

"Who do you think will win the Kosovo War?"

"I haven't the slightest idea."

"Rick is completely neutral about everything," says Captain Renault, finishing off Pocahontas. "And that takes in the field of women."

Overhead we hear the roar of propeller engines as another plane takes off from Traian Vuia International Airport, and it is then I realize that if they're Conrad Veidt and Claude Rains, I must be Humphrey Bogart. I look over at poor Jim. He's become Ilsa Lund, aka Swedish actress Ingrid Bergman. Yet somehow he/she still wears Jim's gray fedora. Wow, what a dame. (Unfortunately I think like Bogie, too.) Time to pull a .38 out of my evening jacket and get this scene moving, but unfortunately I don't have a gun.

"Listen, you mugs, this time I'll narrate." I take a final drag from the cigarette. "I've been abandoned by every dame I ever loved. Even my own mother. But like a fool I went crawling back to her. I had to know if she was all right. Had to reassure her that everything had turned out just swell." I grimace at Major Strasser. "Wanna know the first thing she said to me? 'Whether you were a girl or a boy, I had to get as far away from you as possible.' "

Overhead we hear the roar of propeller engines as another plane takes off from Casablanca bound for freedom.

"The plane to Lisbon?" says Captain Renault. "You would like to be on it?"

"Why, what's in Lisbon?"

"A clipper back to America? I've often speculated on why you didn't stay put in America. Did you abscond with ten million in

US Treasury Bills? Dally with a Wall Street trader—and renege? I like to think that you killed a man. It's the romantic in me."

"It's a combination of all three," I say, raising my eyebrows for emphasis. "You might say I've been trying to outrun a long story, starting with the circumstances of my birth. Wall Street is only a small part of it."

"What in heaven's name brings you to Timişoara?"

"My health. I came for the waters."

"What waters? There are no waters in Timişoara."

By now, I think it's odd that Captain Renault tries to confuse me. He knows as well as I do that Timişoara is situated on the western side of Romania, bordered by the Mureş and Tisa Rivers, the Danube River, and the Banat Mountains. I pause before speaking.

"I was misinformed."

"You weren't always so misinformed," says Major Strasser, once again taking charge of the interview. "We have a complete dossier on you. Richard Blaine, age 47, cannot return to Choctaw Country. The reason is a little vague. We know what you did in Japan in 1993, Mr. Blaine. Also we know why you left Jordan in 1994. Bringing Russian Vodka to an Arab BBQ, Mr. Blaine?! Really? Don't worry, we're not going to broadcast it."

"Hum, are my eyes really brown?"

"You will forgive my curiosity, Mr. Blaine. The point is, an enemy of Romania has come to Timişoara and we're checking up on anybody who can be of help to us."

"My interest in whether the infamous anthropologist stays or goes is purely a sporting one," I say, nodding at Captain Renault. He smiles back.

"In this case you have no sympathy for the fox, huh?" asks Major Strasser.

"Not particularly. I also understand the point of view of the hound."

"This Peruvian-American has published the foulest lies in his books on indigenous power. The revolution is over! Even now, others continue to publish his stories of a separate reality, and of the possibility of assuming the form of a dog. That is, if one follows the thinking of a misguided anthropologist."

We stare at one another. I'd read Castaneda's books years ago and couldn't help but wonder if I'll shape-shift back into the form of a woman once I'm allowed into Romania.

Suddenly I run out of patience and break character. "Excuse me, officers, but your business is intrigue, mine is tourism. My name is LeAnne Howe. I've come to Romania for tourism. I am not Humphrey Bogart."

"Your name and the name of your contact," says Checkpoint Charlie, no longer Major Strasser. Claude Rains has also disappeared.

By this time, Jim has ceased being the longsuffering Ilsa Lund. "She's not a man," he says forcefully, coming to my rescue. "And I'm not Ilsa. Look out the front door of the building! See those Romanians holding up the sign. They're expecting us. She's a tourist, as am I!"

Welcome to Timișoara, LeAnne Howe, Jim Wilson Tourists

Jim offers Charlie one of Sixkiller's cowpatties. It's dark chocolate made to look like cow poop, chock full of peanuts. "Please sirs, try a bite and look at the sign, we're both visiting a summer camp in Reșița." Then he uses the same damn phrase with Checkpoint Charlie that he used with the Syrian Consulate in Amman in order to get me a Visa to visit Damascus. "Madame-ti mobtar-rif-shi." My wife doesn't know anything. Then for good measure he misquotes Socrates, "She knows nothing except the fact of her ignorance."

I glare at him for a split second, thinking that using Arabic and then Greek seems foolhardy considering we're trying to enter Romania. But strange as it seems, Madame-ti mobtar-rif-shi works on the border guards at Timișoara's Checkpoint just as it did on the Syrian Consulate in 1994. Madame-ti mob-tar-rif-shi must be the modern equivalent of the old Aramaic phrase Abracadabra. Words open doors, break spells, and afford entrance into forbidden lands. We grab our bags and walk across an imaginary line into free Romania. Once out of the building we stand in the sunlight and face our new friends, who are still holding up the welcome sign. My uneasy feeling fades as we shake hands with the organizers of the Center for Complexity Studies. I believe we've passed a kind of cosmic test of the non-ordinary variety, but we're only at the beginning of the journey.

By the time I pile into the back seat of a 1989 VW van scheduled to take us to the Center for Complexity Studies near Reşiţa, I'm exhausted. I've never embodied Humphrey Bogart before. Jim says he'd never wants to embody Ilsa Lund again. "She didn't really love Rick like we are led to believe in the movie."

I look at Jim and mouth, "Told you so."

"Ilsa was secretly thrilled to be leaving Casablanca without Rick."

"You're tired. Forget Ilsa. She goes off with Gary Cooper; remember *For Whom the Bell Tolls*."

Jim nods absentmindedly, then decides to ride in the lead van so he can recline in the back seat and nap. It has been twenty-four hours since we slept. As I watch him walk away, I'm glad he's over being surprised by ghosts, spirits, or embodying movie stars at border crossings. He takes both our bags with him and disappears into the other van.

While the journey is a mere 125 kilometers, not far for an Okie, the trip takes us three hours due to potholes the size of small elephants that we must maneuver around on all Romanian highways and roads. Otherwise we crash. Sorin, our driver, is in charge of swerving around traffic jams, stalled vehicles, broken down Mercedes trucks, and of course cars that have flat run out of petrol in the middle of the road. When I ask my seatmates Vlad, Dragos, and Alina about renting a car and driving to Bran

Castle, this seems like a hilarious idea to them. The Romanians near laugh themselves silly.

Alina says, "You would die on our terrible roads." She's a graduate student at the Romanian Academy, Institute of Geodynamics.

After the merriment dies down, Vlad says he would like to ask me a personal question. He speaks English fluently. I speak *no* Romanian.

"Professor, you are really an American Indian?"

"Yes, Choctaw."

"I like reading about the Indians, but I never hear of Choctaws until they announce you are coming." Vlad is very earnest and I immediately trust him. "Someday I would like to come to the US."

"Our tribal headquarters are in Durant, Oklahoma. You're welcome in our home anytime. Homestays are a way of life in Choctaw Country."

Vlad is about six feet tall and very thin with a mop of thick brown hair and hazel eyes that twinkle when he smiles. "Which Native books have been translated into Romanian?" I ask, turning around to push open the back wing windows to let in fresh air.

"There are few translated into Romanian."

"Jim and I have brought several books by American Indian authors to leave at the Center for Complexity Studies, but they're all in English. I have a paperback of Louise Erdrich's *Love Medicine* in my suitcase. You may have it."

"I read now *Journey to Ixtlan*, it is in English," says Vlad confidently. "Carlos Castaneda is fantastic. Before I study *The Teachings of Don Juan* I know nothing about Yaqui people. Does your tribe use the peyote?"

"Well, some Choctaw probably do, but it's not one of our traditions. Nor was it a Yaqui tradition." I hesitate for a moment, choosing my words carefully. "You know, Carlos Castaneda was most likely writing fiction. Don Juan wasn't necessarily real. He was a composite character. Castaneda himself was also a controversial figure. He died earlier this year in April."

"What do you mean?"

"He was born in Peru, and while he became a citizen it's possible he misunderstood tribal traditions in the US. Or, maybe he invented the whole story."

Now Vlad is courteous but firm. "Carlos Castaneda was a well-trained anthropologist and a leading authority on the Yaqui. He understood what Don Juan, the shaman, was showing him. There are alternative realities all around us; as scientists we must learn about them."

"Yes, I know, but Castaneda was writing fiction," I say firmly.

Vlad becomes very animated as he defends Castaneda. Now a strong wind whistles through the window of the van. I strain to hear Vlad's voice. It's quavering, and I realize now that he didn't know Castaneda had passed away.

"Don Juan teaches us that 'death is our only wise adviser,' " says Vlad. "This is complex because life and death and multiple realms of Otherness exist simultaneously. That is the purpose of our summer seminar: to understand, and embrace, Otherness in nature. Separate realities. If we can do this, perhaps it means we can prevent future wars. Foster new research for humankind. Professor, you are teaching on the production of the sacred. Tribal peoples understand these realms. What you are teaching is much like Don Juan's teachings, don't you agree?"

I didn't agree, but Alina, Dragos, and Sorin are listening and it's clear they agree with Vlad. He's obviously intelligent, passionate, and reads all the books he has access to. He also has strong opinions that he's willing to support in the face of criticism, a great combination for an academic.

"May I ask, what is your area of research for your doctorate?"

"Physics. I'm at the Institute of Geodynamics of the Romanian Academy, science branch."

"Ah, now I understand your interest in sacred spaces."

"The production of it," he says, smiling mischievously. "I'm interested in the manifestations of entities whose original forms have changed. The possibilities anyway."

"Shape shifting."

He smiled.

I can feel the tension between us evaporate and we ride the rest of the way to Raul Alb in silence. I reach back in my memory for Carlos Castaneda and his writings while the graduate students doze. I remember that he wrote something profound about silence and saving energy. And that he'd formed a cult in LA.

We finally arrived in Reșița and attended the orientation for the seminar. Jim and I and the other academics stayed at Raul Alb, White River Leisure Centre camp, where all the lectures would be held. Many of the seminar faculty came from universities in Bucharest, others from EU countries—a social scientist from Greece, an anthropologist from Belgium, a science fiction writer from Italy, and two leading Romanian physicists, the seminar organizers, and Jim and me. Lectures covered topics such as: "Fractals in Natural Science"; "Astro-Bio-Geodynamics, a Science for the III Millennium"; "A Virtual Reality into a Virtual Space"; "Let's Experiment: How to Organize a Personal Laboratory"; "Family Policies, Family Place"; and "Rituals of the Sacred." I told stories of the earthwork cultures, the Choctaw's Mother Mound, Nanih Waiya, Native architecture, agronomy, star stories.

"Native stories helped to sustain the settlers who landed on our shores. It's through our stories they learned to grow indigenous foods of the New World." I noted that Vlad, Dragos, Alina, and Sorin took extensive notes during my session, which started to feel like a job talk. Considering how impoverished Romania was under communism, I began to understand why so many graduate students were reading Carlos Castaneda. They asked leading questions like, "What is the secret to the survival of American Indians?" "Stories," I said. "And the will for daily living."

"But what of the stories when the original form has changed?" asked Vlad.

I smiled. "Maybe I can answer that by asking you to give the definition of fractals."

"A fractal," said Vlad obligingly, "is a mathematical set that has a fractal dimension that usually exceeds its topological dimension and may fall between the integers, that is, between the whole numbers. Fractals are typically self-similar patterns where 'self-similar' means they are the same from near as from far."

"If fractals exceed," I said, "a form of change, but what we experience of them remains the same from near or far, does that not solve the question of stories whose original form has changed? What we experience of them is the same from near as from far. "

Vlad looked at me for a long while, but said nothing. I suspected he was thinking I was nuts trying to use the language of math as a way to understand indigenous stories. (Perhaps not even a noun could save me now.)

The second Tuesday of the seminar we traveled back to Reşiţa for an afternoon meal. The city was bustling with traffic. We then drove to Timişoara, the capital of Timis County, to tour some of the sites. Timişoara is an enigmatic place, and the site of a spontaneous protest that began on December 16, 1989, in response to the eviction of bishop László Tőkés from the Church of Romania. The protest fueled the Romanian Revolution of 1989, overthrowing General Secretary of the Romanian Communist Party, Nicolae Ceauşescu, and marking the end of communist era in Romania. Nine days after the protest began, Nicolae Ceauşescu and his wife, Elena, were shot by a firing squad. Considering what the country had been through, it's clear why Vlad is so adamant that Indigenous peoples and indigenous epistemologies are his hope for the future. He needs a new story about his homeland, but one of his making.

As we prepared for a farewell party and bonfire the last night of the seminar, I learned that the Raul Alb had been one of the most popular recreation sites in the country in the communist era. In 1998 it was bleak, austere, and neglected. There were no towels, and there were no blankets on the twin beds, so we piled our clothes over us at night to stay warm. Each morning we ate green peppers and radishes for breakfast, but the fresh bread and hot tea made it a feast. I'd long been persuaded by those who say it's through travel that we learn more about ourselves than we do of the "Other." How easy it would be to lose sight of this leaning into whatever common gestures we can find for comfort, like the sharing of food.

Over the course of the ten-day seminar, I did a great deal of shape shifting, especially as I was repeatedly asked about American Indians and Carlos Castaneda.

Encounter 34: "Are you a real Native American?"

"Yes, Choctaw."

"I read about the Yaqui shaman in a book by Carlos Castaneda."

"Have a chocolate cowboy hat. They're made by real Cherokees."

Encounter 43: "Are you an real Indian?"

"Yes, Choctaw."

"Carlos Castaneda writes about the real Indians, the Yaqui."

"I know nothing except the fact of my ignorance. Have a chocolate cowboy boot. They're made by real Cherokees living in Ada."

Encounter 52: "Are you a Native American?"

"Yes, Choctaw."

"I read about the Yaqui Indians."

"I know, in a book by Carlos Castaneda. It's a Tribalography."

"But didn't you say in your lecture that Native stories, no matter what form they take (novel, poem, drama, memoir, film, history) seem to pull all the elements together of the storyteller's tribe, meaning the people, the land, multiple characters and all their manifestations and revelations, and connect these in past, present, and future milieu? Present, and future milieu means a world that includes non-Indians."

"So, you were listening! Have a chocolate cowboy hat. They're made by a Cherokee businesswoman in Ada."

Encounter 61: "Are you truly a Native Indian?"

"Yes, Choctaw."

"I read about Don Juan, the Yaqui shaman."

"Everything is everything? Have my last chocolate Pocahontas-on-a-stick. She's made by Edna Sixkiller, a Cherokee entrepreneur."

Encounter 70: "Are you sure you're a real American Indian?"

"Not always. Often I'm Humphrey Bogart."

"I read about the Yaqui, is Humphrey Bogart a Yaqui too?"

"Yes. 'Everything exists and everything will happen and everything is alive and everything is planned and everything is a mystery, and everything is dangerous, and everything is a mirage, and everything touches everything, and everything is everything, and everything is very, very strange.'"

And I finally did meet Carlos Castaneda. It was just before twilight on our last night at Raul Alba, a few hours before the bonfire. I'd gone for a quick swim in the river so that in case I was ever questioned again, I could say I'd experienced the waters in Romania. Carlos Castaneda was swimming there, too. As he climbed out of the water and onto the floating wooden boat dock, he walked toward me and stood not more than five feet away.

Castaneda was taller than I imagined, with a mop of thick brown hair. His hazel eyes twinkled when he smiled. He looked very thin in bathing trunks, each one of his ribs was showing.

"You can't outrun your birth Mother's story," he said, flatly.

"How did you know about my birth mother?" I asked in a small voice.

"Shape-shifting at the airport," he said.

I nodded slowly.

"She didn't abandon you when you were born, she died when you were born. Imagine, she had to walk out of that home for unwed Indian women as Other. Excluded. Different and indifferent. Who do you think bequeathed you the strength to become the Other, a mouth with fingers that will write the stories of Grandmother of Birds, a fierce warrior, baseball players, dying soldiers, and even Humphrey Bogart?"

We remained silent for a long while. In the muted light, words did not come easily. Eventually the sun set in a blazing red sky. I asked him if he was going to live here long.

He shrugged. "No wind tonight. Nothing but glittering stars."

Yaa Jordan, Yaa 'Ayouni

On a cold clear night in Amman, Jordan, November 1993, I died. The time was 10 p.m. It was not the first time, nor the last. Roll film.

OPENING SCENE, FADE IN:
Hubble Space Telescope image of the blue green orb, Earth, from outer space. CAMERA zooms in to a broad flat map of the Middle East, then into a medium shot of a map of Jordan. Photomontage of Amman images, past and present, with its seven prominent hills, creates a ten-second tease as the voice of the narrator describes moving to Jordan.

LEANNE (V.O.)
On Halloween 1993, I fly from Washington, DC, to Amman. Within a month, I go on Jordan TV to talk about American Indians and human rights (something my experiences in Japan had prepared me for). Later, I begin designing clothes with an Egyptian tailor in Amman. On Christmas Eve I go to the Syrian

Embassy to apply for a visa to enter Damascus, Syria. The application asks for my religious affiliation. I write that I practice Choctaw religion. Who knew the Syrian Embassy's Visa clerk in Amman, an Alawite from the ruling party in Syria, was schooled in American Indian religions.

CUT TO:

SYRIAN EMBASSY CLERK

(WAVING APPLICATION)
This not religion! Refused.

CAMERA CLOSE-UP of Syrian Embassy Clerk's moustache on her upper lip.

LEANNE
You know the pharmacy has products for that.

SMASH CUT TO:
FANTASY—IMAGES OF THE NEW WORLD CIRCA 1392 WITH NATIVES PLANTING HERBS; HOSTING PARTIES; DRINKING STEAMING CUPS OF CHOCOLATE CHILI COCOA; MEANWHILE THOUSANDS OF PEOPLE WAIT IN LINE OUTSIDE THE SYRIAN EMBASSY IN AMMAN, TRYING TO OBTAIN VISAS INTO SYRIA.

LEANNE

(LOOKS DIRECTLY INTO CAMERA)
I tried framing a rhetorical argument about religions in the New World—before contact. It didn't work. Sadly, I must now find another way to Damascus.

CUT TO:
WIDE ANGLE POV of Amman with its white stone buildings, seven prominent hills, and desert landscape.

LEANNE (V.O.)

Before the Middle East, before Jordan, before the
incident at the Syrian Embassy, I'd long been attracted
to the idea of death and what's beyond our recognition
that those at death's door witness. Does the earth itself
fade away as we encounter our origins, or is it someone
else's origins we see? I die three times during the year
I am in the Middle East, and each death buries much
deeper into the past than the previous dying. I suppose
I'm looking for an answer to a simple question: Why
am I here?

CUT TO:

WIDE ANGLE POV of Amman with its white stone buildings,
seven prominent hills, and desert landscape. Zoom in to a
close-up of two women in a pastry shop.

FADE OUT

And then suddenly the story was here.

My friend Mindy and I stopped at Chez Hilda Pâtisserie
and Confiserie in Sweifieh on the west side of Amman to pick
up a box of French pastries and hand-dipped chocolates. Garth
Brooks' "Friends in Low Places" filled Mindy's Cadillac as we
tooled around the city. In February 1994 it was still possible to
"drag Amman," the way that teenagers drag Main in small towns
throughout America. At the Third Circle we headed west toward
King Talal Square when one of us said, "Why don't we go to
Beirut today, you know they have great restaurants, and we're
not all that far away."

Only Texans and Oklahoma Indians say such things. Mindy
was a Texan, and I'm Choctaw. After we met in Jordan sometime
in December, we became fast friends. One of the reasons for that
friendship is that we shared a warped vision of space and time.
So when Mindy suggested we drive across two Arab countries
for a good meal in Lebanon, it seemed like a normal thing to do.

My journal notes from the trip begin with:

Freaky warm day in mid-February

Seventy degrees Fahrenheit

Clear blue skies, a kind of day that fosters adventure...

Surprise. 188 miles to Beirut from Amman, by car. Must cross Syria.

"Friends in Low Places" played for a second time as we made our way across Amman, missing pedestrians and the occasional goat or sheep that meandered onto the street. At Highway 35, we drove north toward Jerash munching on cream-filled croissants and chocolates, singing along with Garth, determined to make Beirut, Lebanon, or bust.

Another ten miles into the journey we screeched to a halt and waited for a herd of camels to cross 35 (no one calls it "35" but map-reading-Americans). Not stopping for Bedouin herding sheep, goats, or camels across a highway would be the arrogance of unrestrained power. Besides, Bedouin have grazing rights, meaning they go anywhere in the kingdom where there is suitable fodder for their herds.

Camels safely off the road, car in drive, we again headed toward our destination.

Here, I should say something grand about Jerash. Fifty three miles from Amman, it's a magnificent archaeological site of the ancient Greco-Roman city of Gerasa, supposedly established by Alexander the Great in 331 BCE as he made his way across Egypt into Syria and onto Mesopotamia. Look on the map at the distance from Egypt to Mesopotamia. Alexander did some heavy-duty touring (*uh-hem*, pillaging), but recent excavations show that Jerash was inhabited during the Bronze Age, long before his arrival. It had built a hippodrome with ten starting gates and a seating area that could accommodate 15,000 spectators. A far cooler factoid about Jerash is that it's the birthplace of Nicomachus, a mathematician born in about 60 CE who wrote of the mystical properties of numbers. Nicomachus was best known for his *Introduction to Arithmetic*.

But forget Jerash.

We were on a quest for the "Paris of the East," to stroll the Corniche along Lebanon's Mediterranean coastline. See Pigeon Rock. Mostly, I wanted a big plate of *Kibbeh nayyeh*, something I hadn't found in Amman. *Kibbeh nayyeh* is minced raw lamb, mixed with bulgur, spices, and drizzled with virgin olive oil and fresh mint. Supposedly the dish originated in Aleppo, Syria. I'd first eaten it at Hedary's Mediterranean Restaurant in Fort Worth, Texas, when I was living there and working in Dallas. Mr. Hedary, a Lebanese Christian, was a master at preparing the kibbeh, and I always ordered it with fresh baked Arabic bread, garlicky *hummus bi-tahini*, *batinjan mtabble*, and a glass of wine. Perhaps my love of the Middle East really begins at Hedary's Restaurant, talking with Mr. Hedary and his Lebanese customers and seeing posters of their homelands.

As we continued driving northward, Jordan's landscape changed to undulating fields of rich brown earth, tufts of pines, and groves of olive trees. Even the air changed, as the forests of Irbid renewed the atmosphere. In the north of Jordan, the smog disappears, the air smells crisp and alive. As we approached the town of Ramtha, near the border with Syria, Mindy pulled the car over and stopped.

"Still game?"

"I don't even have to think about it."

She lit up a cigarette and inhaled thoughtfully. "We're halfway to Damascus. Once we hit *Tariiq Beirut*, the highway on the western side of city, it's only 53 miles more to Beirut."

"Beirut's my hometown." I said it perky, as if I were making a Cheerios breakfast commercial.

Mindy laughed, "Whaddayoumean? You've never been to Beirut."

"I know. But I lost something there, I'm sure of it."

"Really?"

"Of course not, but I feel like I did." Now I was laughing too, as I searched through the CDs for Willie Nelson's *Live From Austin, Texas*.

"I hear ya," she said. "First time I traveled to Cairo I felt like I knew it. Who knows why. Got your US passport and immigration visa from the Hashemite Kingdom of Jordan?"

"Next to my heart."

"Me too." Mindy started the V8 engine and spun gravel as we pulled onto the road again. We buckled up in case the Jordan police stopped us before we crossed into Syria. Willie Nelson crooned, "Crazy," and I must have flashed an anguished face because Mindy said in a comforting voice, "We'll get in."

"*Inshallah*," I said.

"Just don't make any more Syrian Embassy visa clerks mad."

CUT TO:

WIDE ANGLE POV of cars in line at the Jordan-Syria border crossing. Close up on the men's faces driving the cars and commercial trucks.

FADE OUT

When our turn came, and we had no visas, a guard with a sidearm and a Kalashnikov assault rifle waved us into the parking lot of the border station. We walked into the sandy-colored building and stood in line behind the others folks with visa problems. (Maybe they'd had trouble with the Syrian visa clerk in Amman.) A large color portrait of Hafez al-Assad, President of Syria, hung directly above the row of border patrol agents. It was the only thing of color in the entire beige building. Al-Assad (the lion) was born to a poor Alawite family of the Kalbiyya tribe in Qardaha, Syria. He had been a pilot in the Syrian Air Force and over the years rose to power in a series of coups against his mentors and friends. In 1971 he became prime minister. Two years later, president. One thing he did right, however, was to change the Syrian constitution to guarantee equal status for women. (Hence the very powerful Alawite female visa clerk at the Syrian Embassy in Amman.)

In the queue, men were talking a mile a minute, border guards with Kalashnikovs trekked in and out the front door, and outside a car horn honked sporadically. For a moment, I studied the portrait of Hefaz al-Assad and considered whether I could make love to such a man. (I do that with portraits of dictators.) His head was misshapen with a forehead the size of a hand-mirror. Reedy lips. No, I couldn't imagine it.

I turned back to the task at hand. This time I didn't write Choctaw on the visa application and instead checked "Christian." Although I'm not a Christian, I wanted to see Damascus, and someday Aleppo, and all the places in between. Telling the truth at the embassy in Amman had met with failure. Time for a new strategy.

Jews, Christians, and Muslims are "people of the book," meaning though they may go to war with one another, they acknowledge each other's beliefs and practices. East Asians and South Asians, not so much. American Indians not at all. They don't know us. Well, I take that back; they do know stereotypes. For decades Hollywood produced hundreds of movies with Indians in headdresses.

Today, Arabs in keffiyehs fighting the US military have replaced images of Plains Indians fighting the US Cavalry. The fact that Arabs identify with Indians and *not* John Wayne isn't surprising. We've both been enemies of the United States. Recall US General Philip Sheridan's snappy comeback in 1869 to Comanche Chief Tosawi, "The only good Indians I ever saw were dead."

Perhaps that's why the trinket shop in Amman, *al-hindi al-humr*, the Red Indian Shop, sold beads and handmade bone chokers from China.

CUT TO:

MEDIUM SHOT of Howe posed in front of the *al-hindi al-humr* shop getting her picture taken.

FADE OUT

I don't pretend to hold the moral high ground either. I'm standing in line masquerading as a Christian in order to scoot through Syria and cross the Anti-Lebanon Mountains for a plate of kibbeh nayyeh. Wackiness all around.

Mindy was confident and seemed to deftly handle the visa situation that would, hopefully get us into Syria. She spoke Arabic with authority and showed the Syrian officer our passports, Jordanian visas, her Jordanian work permit, and the 1989 Cadillac Seville's vehicle registration papers from Florida. I couldn't really follow all that was said, but I understood a word here and there.

"*Mowjudeh?*" He asked. Is she here?

"*Na'am,*" said Mindy, turning to look at me.

The officer stared at me for a moment. I knew from Mindy's look it was my turn to speak. He had humorous brown eyes, wavy black hair; a handsome face. I judged him to be in the early 30s. He looked at my American passport, then at me. He must have been wondering if I was an Arab with an English last name. *Long black hair, dark brown eyes. No Hijab but modestly dressed. Must be Christian.*

I got this look all the time. After four months in Jordan I'd come to understand why. I resembled 99 percent of the Arabs in the *Bilaad ash Sham*; the general name for the whole Levant, Greater Syria. Black hair, brown eyes, olive complexion. The experience reminded me again that what we manifest on the outside is the identity we live with. Throughout the region I was read as Arab until I opened my mouth. But on the inside I was the same woman who left America for Jordan, though perhaps not. I could feel my life in Jordan changing me ever-so-slightly with each new experience. I stared at the officer and waited one more heartbeat before speaking.

"*Salam aleikum.*" I said, smiling.

Question solved. I read his eyes, *Amerikiya.* He turned back to Mindy. More negotiations.

"*Muffeeshe?*" He asked. There is nothing? "*Anjad?*" Seriously?

More talking. But I think that he said, "You have no more papers. Seriously?"

I zoned out for a moment and noted that the officer was nursing a small steaming glass of *shai*, Arabic tea. It's made by boiling fresh tea leaves to release the aromatic flavors. The amber liquid is then poured through a sieve into individual tea glasses. I drink it *wasat*, medium, which means with a heaping teaspoon of sugar stirred in. Delicious. Makes you throw rocks at commercial tea bags.

Sometime during my idleness the conversation turned. Tone, banter, and words like *tayib*, okay, all signaled that we were going to get two "on-arrival" visas.

Another series of short questions.

"*Aind'nah*" said Mindy. We have it.

"*Mumtaz.*" Excellent.

More chatting. *Caza-caza*, etc. Mindy paid for the visas.

"*Shukran*," said Mindy. "*Ma'assalama!*"

Chiming in I added, "*Ma'assalama.*" Then, "*Yallah* bye-bye," a colloquial phrase often used by Lebanese. My first attempt at flirting in the Middle East.

Back in the car, Mindy and I celebrated by eating the last of the croissants. "You did it, hooray!" I wiped powdered sugar off my mouth.

Mindy closed the empty box. "He was nice." She threw her head back and laughed. "I do need to get some kind of official Jordanian paper for my car..." she stopped in mid-sentence. "Do you think Brownsville's Port of Entry would give visas to Mexicans wanting to cross into Texas?"

We belly laughed at the very idea and then fell into a somber reverie. We both knew the truth of racism against Mexicans in

Texas and Oklahoma, and across America.

"As a country we're not kind. Look at the histories of Blacks, Mexicans, Japanese, Arabs, and Indians."

"I know," said Mindy, "we're such hypocrites. Once I believed what Emma Lazarus wrote. 'Give me your tired, your poor, your huddled masses yearning to breathe free.' Do you think it was ever true of America?"

I gave her one of my sideway glances, "Forget Emma Lazarus." Only I didn't say "forget."

Disaster Braking On the Road to Damascus

We drove a short distance to Daara, a small city just inside Syria. Everywhere there were large posters plastered on the buildings and billboards, signs of Hafez al-Assad. We were headed to the oldest continuously inhabited city in the world, Damascus, run by a man whose lion head was everywhere. From Al Sham our plan was to head west on Tariiq Beirut, the road to Beirut. I know it sounds crazy to cross Syria and the Anti-Lebanon Mountains just for a great Lebanese meal, but it was 1994. Most important, we had good transportation. Lebanon's civil war had ended in 1990 and the country was rebuilding, although Syria still controlled Lebanon's domestic and foreign affairs. Since 1993, Syria began playing the "Hezbollah card," meaning they wouldn't restrain the Shiite Islamic militant group from attacking Israeli troops in Lebanon. But that probably wouldn't affect us. And, most important, we had good transportation.

Sometimes I look back and ask myself why we ever considered driving from Amman to Beirut. I don't know why anymore than I can tell you why from 1946-1948 Sir Wilfred Thesiger crossed and re-crossed 250,000 miles of the Empty Quarter, the largest body of sand in the world, barefoot. I don't know why Sir Richard Francis Burton had himself circumcised so he could go on the hajj in 1853 dressed as Mirza Abdullah. He first traveled to Medina, then to the sacred city of Mecca and sketched the mosque and the Ka'bah, the holiest of shrines. He could have been killed as an imposter. I don't know why Gertrude Bell traveled across Arabia six times in twelve years. Or why Freya Stark trekked by camel into the western wilderness of Iran in 1930, going where no European woman had gone before.

All I know is that I was obsessed with the idea of crossing a landscape of desert and mountains, where pungent roses bloom fitfully in rawest sunlight. Besides, thousands of Jordanians cross Syria into Lebanon every day. It was only 188 miles and we had good transportation. Mindy's 1989 Cadillac Seville had been recently serviced. It was the same reliable car she'd had shipped from Florida to Egypt and then to Aqaba, and I couldn't help but smile as we sped along the Syrian highway with a license plate that read "Florida, Sunshine State."

After a few miles across the windswept semi-arid steppe, we stopped talking, mesmerized by the scenery and the travelers and vehicles on the road. Syria has the funniest looking three-wheeler trucks. They're a chopped and squeezed version of a Ford Ranger pickup, with a single miniature tire in the front and decorated with surrey fringe around the cab.

To say that all was right with the world (although it damn well wasn't) explains how I was feeling at that moment. I pulled my briefcase out of the backseat and began writing notes about the trip, paying no attention to the lonely stray sheep that had propelled itself onto the road and stopped there, obviously attempting suicide.

Mindy swerved and jammed the brakes, the car skidded sideways, burning rubber twenty feet or so before coming to a full stop. She'd barely missed the poor creature. My torso and I flew toward the windshield but my seatbelt held. It was my briefcase that took the brunt of the crash. We exchanged wide-eyed glances. Gathering our wits, we pulled off the road and examined the Cadillac and tires. No visible damage, nothing seemed amiss so we continued on. This time I was driving.

Obtaining a visa into Lebanon in 1994 was going to be tricky. In the mid-1980s, America passed a law that forbade our travel to Lebanon. In 1994 the travel ban was still in force. If we could get in we'd have to ask the border agent to stamp a piece of paper, rather than our passports, so there would be no record on our US passports of our coming or going. This was a common practice among countries in the region, including Israel. As we talked about the visa problems, Mindy pulled a battered letter out of her purse. Written in classical Arabic by the owner of the tourism services company she worked for, it read something like, "Please allow travel agent Mindy Smith into Lebanon to establish business connections between Beirut tour operators and my company."

"*Yaa Allah*," said Mindy. "This letter might get me into Lebanon. Because you've got no excuse to go to Lebanon, you can be my assistant."

I drove on.

We reached Damascus round 5:30. Dusk. The desert air was growing cold. I wished I'd brought my red warrior coat; it was back in Amman. The sun was sinking into a haze of smog, becoming a large orange bulb that gave no heat and very little light.

CUT TO:

CAMERA MEDIUM SHOT of roadside benzene station with a large poster of Hafez al-Assad painted on the outside of a small beige building.

FADE OUT

Unlike most Syrians, the President of Syria never smiled. An attendant for the pumps came out of the building wearing a faded blue-and-white-checkered keffiyeh.

"*Salam aleikum.*"

"*Aleikum Salam.*"

"*Biddi benzene*," I asked.

He topped up our gas tank and washed the windows. I'd never seen a keffiyeh that wasn't red and white or black and white.

"*Tehki Arabi,* good?" he said.

"*Ma ba'arif ehki Arabi.* I don't speak Arabic." I smiled. "*Shway,* little." Then I paid him in Jordanian dinars and asked in English if he could change it into Syrian pounds. He hesitated then said, "Okay." (This was a full service operation.)

When he came back with the change he bent down and talked to us through the car window. His name was Ali. He had hazel eyes and a small moustache. He was tall and his hands were calloused and stained from working on cars. He asked if we were Americans. Mindy began speaking Arabic with him, as I'd reached the limits of my language abilities. Ali invited us to his home for dinner. He said his younger sister was getting married later that evening, and we were most welcome to attend the wedding. This happens all the time in Arab countries. Arabs are famous for their hospitality and generosity and will gladly share a bountiful feast with strangers. They'll go hungry for days afterward and never think twice about it. I've taken tea in the homes of shopkeepers, taxi drivers, the owner of a flourmill outside of Madaba, and with poor Bedouin herders around Wadi Araba in the south. Glubb Pasha, the British commanding general of the former Transjordan Arab Legion, thought that the "medieval conception of chivalry came to Europe from the Arabs at the time of the Crusades."

Mindy explained that we were expected in Beirut that evening. We got out of the car thanked him profusely, saying a thousand blessings on his family. Suddenly two women in flowing black veils walked up to the benzene station and began selling bundles of fresh herbs. Then a camel driver and his camel appeared out of nowhere. Man and camel zigzagged among the trucks and cars in line for fuel.

Although Beirut was our destination, I was momentarily lost in competing visions of Syria as I waited for Mindy. Poverty and generosity all around, but it was the city I had imagined. In the distance I could see the lights of Damascus twinkling. Dusk was ebbing. Previously denied a visa into Syria, I yearned more than ever to be in the old city. I must have gone into a kind of traveler's trance because in my mind's eye I saw the Umayyad Mosque, one of the largest in the world. I'd only been able to study it in books. Inside the mosque was the head of John the Baptist. Outside in the gardens near the mosque, the great Arab leader Ṣalāḥ ad-Dīn was buried. In 1187 he'd led the Islamic re-conquest that defeated the Crusaders. He was such a successful leader that he united Yemen in the south, Egypt, Syria, Mesopotamia, the Hejaz, and parts of Northern Africa under his sultanate. Yet he died a poor man in Damascus in 1193. He'd given away most of his wealth to the people in the lands of his sultanate. Standing in the parking lot of benzene station, I felt certain I'd see Ṣalāḥ ad-Dīn's fire still burning if I were to climb to the top Mount Qasion.

"Yaa Ṣalāḥ ad-Dīn," I said his name properly in Arabic. "The truest warrior and leader."

"Ready for Beirut?" asked Mindy, abruptly pulling me out of the trance.

"*Ana hadr*, ready. But we must return to Damascus."

Mindy finished her cigarette and opened her car door. "We will. There's more than one way to skin a visa!"

We pulled out of the station and veered west onto *Tariiq Beirut*, the highway. A few miles outside of Damascus we stopped at a great Syrian-Lebanese restaurant. It had an expansive menu, so we ordered grilled lamb, *mezze* salads, Arabic coffee and fruits for dessert. Sitting across the room was a man and his three wives. They were all young by American standards. He appeared to be in his early forties, while the women seemed younger. They wore black veils, gorgeous black chiffon gowns and black high heels that clicked against the marble floor. They would occasionally flit around the room like small blackbirds. I had the feeling they were sister-wives. We presumed they were Saudi, and I couldn't help but wonder what it might be like to be the third wife. I remember my birth mother said she cleaned house for a

Choctaw old lady named Kompellabe. This was shortly after I was born. Kompellabe's Choctaw husband had also married her sister, and they all lived together in one large house in McAlester, Oklahoma. My mother said she felt like they wanted her to be the third wife, so she quit them. No scene I will ever write for film could evoke how my mother felt about her life. Though she was the embodiment of stoic, she shuddered at the thought of being a third wife.

Mindy finished her cigarette and we left the restaurant and got back into the car. She started the engine and put her foot on the brake. It went all the way to the floorboard. We were not going anywhere.

My journal notes from the trip end with my second death:

Restaurant owner sent for his nephew.

Two hours later a young man arrived.

Brake fluid gone, gaskets? A Line?!

We needed a tow, slept in the car.

Never made it to Beirut, or

the old city of Damascus.

Fell asleep in the backseat

Stopped breathing. Died. Learned nothing.

Revived by a stranger

that pumped my heart

seventeen times.

No vision, just blue waters.

How I Came To Live in Jordan

I have one photograph of Jim Wilson and me standing in front of a tall grass prairie in the spring of 1994. It was taken in Amman, right outside our flat. We'd had good rains that year and the trellis on the side of the flat was covered with the most fragrant long-stemmed yellow roses I've ever seen. (Fossil evidence suggests that roses flourished at least 32 million years ago.)

CUT TO:

CLOSE-UP shot of ancient soft pink roses that originated in the Northern Hemisphere. Use time-lapse photography as they change color from pink to yellow. Cross cut images of Amman, past and present, with its white stone buildings, seven prominent hills, and desert landscape.

LEANNE (V.O.)

Sometime in the eighteenth century, yellow roses were discovered growing in the Middle East. This caused a buzz among European growers. I think the roses next to our flat are the descendants of the first wild, golden-petal rose that changed into something new. That is the story of the Middle East. Everyone that comes here dies and is reborn with a desire to become something new. Maybe that is the sacred message of the land.

FADE OUT

I have never been faithful to any one lifestyle or place. I've wanted to know as many lands as possible, which doesn't negate my love for my tribe's original homeland. Deciphering life in Jordan began on November 1, 1993, when Jim Wilson received a Fulbright-Hayes Scholarship to Amman, Jordan. He'd lived in the Middle East for nearly ten years in the 1980s, and this return was a kind of homecoming for him. I had some idea of what it might be like to live in Jordan after we had gone on a study tour of Israel, Palestine, and Jordan in 1992. When the offer came, we decided that ten months in Jordan would be good for both of us. He would conduct research for his dissertation; I would write a novel. Shortly after he left for Jordan in September 1993, I traveled to Washington, DC, and worked for a month as a Native American intern at the Smithsonian Institution. My project was to read over Cyrus Byington's nineteenth-century letters, diaries, and note cards on the Choctaw language. I wanted to know if Byington's thinking evolved on certain Choctaw words and concepts. Byington was a Presbyterian missionary who settled in the Choctaw Nation in 1820 and translated the first five books of the Bible into the Choctaw language. Ironically I was going to live, at least for a time, in the land where many of those stories he translated had taken place. The stories were used to change Choctaws into something different, and now I wondered if I was becoming something different in this new land...

Journal notes from my first week in Amman:

Arrived at 1 am

Jim was waiting for me

at Queen Alia International Airport.

His hair looked a little grayer than

when he left Iowa two months ago

Air travel from DC smooth. No problems.

Flight attendant thought I was Jordanian

She brought me the customs declaration form written in Arabic

Huda was my seatmate. Lebanese.

I hope we remain friends

November 3, 1993

Sill Jetlagged. Problems sleeping.

Waking with the Muazzin's first call to prayer.

Spellbound.

We lived in a large flat on a hillside in Jubaiha overlooking Jordan University. Sheep and goats regularly grazed on the prairie in front of the flat, and I assumed life in Amman would be pastoral and uneventful, but I was wrong. Before my first week had ended, Moona and Musallim called and invited us to go to Irbid for mansef with Moona's family. It's one of those complicated six degrees of Kevin Bacon stories. Moona was the half-sister of Rahim al-Webdah, a friend in Iowa City. Musallim, Moona's husband, worked for the Mukhabaraat in Jordan (think CIA), so we knew it would be ill-advised to ask penetrating questions about King Hussein, or the Jordanian government.

"Moona and Musallim feel obligated to host us because we had Rahim over for dinner many times," Jim said. "You'll enjoy the scenic countryside and it's beautiful in the north."

"I *want* to go," I said.

The next day, M&M picked us up at our flat and we drove in a Range Rover to Irbid with their two younger children. The hour-long drive to Irbid was uneventful and a bit formal. Men in the front seat, women and children in the back. We didn't know each other, so we talked about Rahim.

I was filled with anticipation. Rahim and Moona's father was a hereditary Sheik, and an Imam who'd served as a chaplain in the Jordanian army. He had two wives and twenty-five kids. Rahim was the oldest son of the second wife. I'd never met anyone with twenty-five children before, yet I vowed to stay open and avoided asking questions like "Where do you buy their shoes?" I wasn't about to tear it in another foreign country and repeat the "Fugimoro incident," as it had come to be called by my family.

The family home was colorless and on the outskirts of Irbid. Inside it was lovely, a large compound with gendered spaces, a mudaffa for men, and a mudaffa for women, and a long house of connecting doors. Jim went with Musallim outside to bring in some sacks of groceries from Amman. I went with four of the women into the kitchen and we played word games with food. They wanted to teach me Arabic.

"*Basal.*" Moona said pointing to an onion.

"*Basal*," I repeated.

She pointed to salt. "*Mileh.*"

"*Mileh*," I'd repeat breathing out the "h," as they did.

"*Djaj.*" She pointed to the roast chicken covered in freshly chopped, "*kisbara*," she said.

"Cilantro," I repeated in English.

"*Shoo?*" grinned Moona. What?

"Cilantro is *kisbara.*" We all laughed at my English translation into Arabic, I'd meant to say the opposite.

Just then we were summoned to Umm Rahim's house. (Once a woman has a son she's called Umm followed by her son's name.) Lunch was ready and we washed our hands at a sink and headed for her salon.

SCENE 2, FADE IN:

CAMERA PANS the people and room. A Bedouin rug made from sheep wool and camel hair covers the floor. Large colorful pillows decorate the room. A traditional mensef meal, a Jordanian specialty, is being served on a three-foot-wide silver platter. Cooked lamb mounded over a bed of rice garnished with almonds and parsley, and covered with special sauce of yogurt and *jameed.*

CUT TO:

MEDIUM SHOT of Umm Rahim and her two daughters who are unnamed in the scene. They're reverential and nervous as the venerable old Sheik approaches the salon. LONG SHOT of the Sheik walking with a cane. His back is straight as a rod. He has a white beard, piercing brown eyes and looks like Omar Mukhtar, the Libyan leader who fought the Italian invaders from 1911 until 1931 when Mussolini's forces finally killed him.

CLOSE-UP ON SHEIK, 84, as he enters his second wife's house. He bows on one knee at the door and asks permission to enter. He does not acknowledge anyone else's presence, just hers. He takes her hand.

SHEIK

Salamaat yaa Hajjia, peace on you, oh Pilgrim.

UMM RAHIM

(SMILES AT HER HUSBAND)

Waa aleykum as-salaam, yaa Hajj, And upon you
peace, oh Pilgrim.

CAMERA PANS to Musallim and Moona and each individual
adult member of his family already present in the room. The
Sheik sits down on the floor next to Musallim and makes polite
conversation with the men. Sound mix: "How was the trip from
Amman? What was the news?" Musallim keeps the conversation light-hearted and people laugh as he talks.

SHEIK

(GIVES ARABIC BREAD TO JIM)

CAMERA POV, SHEIK. He sees everyone is relaxed, the mood
happy. In the scene, the Sheik's relatives—men, women, and
children—all talk at once. The Sheik watches Jim Wilson tear
a small piece of Arabic bread and fold it into the size of a large
rose petal.

JIM WILSON

(USES THE BREAD LIKE A SCOOP AND POPS IT IN HIS MOUTH.)

Watch. Now you try it.

CAMERA POV, SHEIK. Zoom in for a close up of LeAnne. She
makes a scoop with her Arabic bread. Puts the fingers of her left
hand together and digs into the platter of rice and almonds as
the others are doing.

LEANNE

(TO THE SHEIK)

Delicious, I've never eaten with my hands. What a
delight!

CUT TO:

MEDIUM SHOT OF the Sheik, it's unclear he understood her. He eyes LeAnne and says something in Arabic about "the people of the book," and everyone in the room stops talking instantly.

CUT TO:

POV LEANNE, CAMERA PANS from her face to all the family members seated in the room.

MUSALLIM

You are eating with your left hand.

LEANNE

Yes. I'm left-handed.

SMASH CUT TO:

FANTASY—HELLISH SCENES FROM THE FUGIMORO INCIDENT IN JAPAN CROSSCUT WITH JORDANIAN FAMILY; Musallim and Jim Wilson jumping up to explain to the Sheik why she eats with her left hand.

SHEIK

(thoughtfully studies his guests)
Khalas. Enough. *Khaliha tu'd ma-na.* She may stay in the room.

FADE OUT

In the film within the story, the road back to Amman was much more lively. We passed white stone buildings along the highway and marveled at sunsets in Jordan, how the fine blowing sand of the Arabian Desert makes the sky at dusk appear to glitter, as if Amman were a fairyland. We'd all loosened up after the left-handed incident. Apparently, throughout the Arab world it is said, "When you eat with your left hand, the devil eats with you. If you don't say '*Bismillah ir-Rahman ir-Rahim,* in the name of God, most Gracious, most Compassionate', before eating or drinking the devil eats with you. If you don't say 'Alhamdulillah, Praise to God', after eating or after drinking, the devil eats with you." I was learning about Jordanian customs, Islamic customs, and what things were *makruh*, offensive.

Since I had already broken all the rules of decorum, I thought I might as well ask Musallim about who he thought were the best and worst Arab leaders in the Middle East. (When would I be in the company of the *Mukhabaraat* again?) I could feel Jim wincing all the way from the front seat of the Range Rover.

Of course Musallim didn't answer but began telling jokes about one Arab leader or another. "Everybody joking this way," he said. He told us the one about Yasser Arafat and Marilyn Monroe, then about Saddam Hussein asking his friends to jump out of airplanes. Usually he told the jokes in Arabic first, Jim and Moona would laugh hardily, and then they'd take turns translating for me. Finally when I asked about Syrian leader Hafez al-Assad, the lion, Musallim hesitated. "It is said even the cats in Syria kiss his hand," he said solemnly. We all laughed loudly.

The next day after the trip to Irbid I came down with a terrible sore throat and high fever. By the evening my fever was 104, and I was hallucinating again—back in a hospital bed in Bethany, Oklahoma, with the dying woman in the next bed. I'm eight and have rheumatic fever. My body concrete, each move a dreadful breaking. The old woman has lung cancer and struggles to breathe. Through fever's veil, I realize that we're related. Twinned. Otherwise why are we together, vanishing in beds of hot sand? I can no longer call out for help and the room goes black. No sound. Out of the story, I walk off-camera, vanquished. There's no more for me to see. It will be thousands and thousands of years before I reach the Bering Strait.

In Jordan I Meet a Cherokee Indian Princess

I swear to the *Almighty* this is true.

So I go to the US Embassy in Amman to check out library

books. At this time it's still possible for Americans living in Amman to use the library. Right up until Fairouz (not her real name), a Jordanian librarian, mentioned Chicago, I was certain her story about her Cherokee Indian grandmother being a descendant of Pocahontas was bullshit. A similar story was told to me in Jerusalem when I met an Israeli shopkeeper.

This is Fairouz's story. "Jiddc, my great grandfather, brought his wife and daughter, my grandmother, from the US home to Jordan, shortly after she was born. 1941, I think. Jeddah, my Cherokee great grandmother, died soon after. She caught a high fever. I asked my family about this many times, but they know nothing more. Sad, no? But I like to remember that I am part Native American, the Cherokee related to Pocahontas. I am proud of the red Indians."

(Silence.)

After a time I thank her for the story. And the remarkable thing was that everything about that story, *sans* Pocahontas, was plausible.

Everyone knows the story of how twelve-year-old Pocahontas saved the life of British Captain John Smith in 1607. Debatable, I know. Yet, fast-forward six years, Pocahontas, captured by the English (for ransom), converts to Christianity, changes her name to Rebecca, marries John Rolfe, has a son Thomas, goes to England in 1617, hobnobs with Royals, becomes sick and dies of a European disease: smallpox.

In the histories written about Pocahontas *cum* Rebecca Rolfe, it should be noted that none of the other English colonists made an issue of Thomas Rolfe's half-bred status. Nor did they object to Thomas Rolfe's marriage to Elizabeth Washington in 1632 on the grounds that he was of mixed race. At that time he was thought of as having royal Native blood. Today most people that claim Pocahontas as their ancestor are people descended from Thomas and Elizabeth Rolfe's daughter Ann, and her husband Peter Elwin. If they do their genealogy homework they must realize that Pocahontas was not Cherokee; her tribe was from the Tidewater region of Virginia.

The story of Pocahontas has taken on mythic proportions and become a literary trope to help settler colonials feel a part of the land they're appropriating. But I think Pocahontas's tribe gets twinned with Cherokees because Virginia and North Carolina are close in proximity. The Cherokees developed a trading partnership with the British *aka* Virginian traders as early as 1690. Cherokee women did marry with men from the Empire. Soon afterwards "princes and princesses" were running around barefoot in the Southeast descended from British fathers and Native mothers. This is the history of contact in America. Claiming a Native identity through ancestry allows non-Indians to own American Indian history, be entitled to it *and* our homelands, yet have no actual responsibility for any of it.

The Night The Infidels Brought Shame to Wadi Musa

My journal notes from December 30:

Off to Petra to spend New Year's Eve in Wadi Musa

Mindy, Saif, Ahmed, and the gang will BBQ lamb. I'll make potato salad. Yum.

Must stop at the Christian liquor store in Jebal Weibdeh.

SCENE 3, FADE IN:

CAMERA DOLLYS AROUND THE TOWN of Wadi Musa, "Spring of Moses," in southern Jordan. Israelis also visit Wadi Musa in Jordan because it's one of the places where the prophet Moses made miracles. Petra, a UNESCO World Heritage Site, is also located outside of Wadi Musa. Tourists from around the world arrive by the thousands.

LEANNE (V.O.)

I'm very sorry for what happened. And while it wasn't *entirely* my fault, I take full responsibility for all the drinking and dancing that occurred in Petra on New Year's Eve, 1994, and for bringing a quart of Stolichnaya to the party. The affair known as "The Night the Infidels Brought Shame to Wadi Musa" begins when Mindy calls to invite Jim and me to a small party to be held in Petra. *Ain-Musa*, the "Spring of Moses," is where purportedly Prophet Moses tapped his cane on a rock and fresh water poured forth. Until now the spring still gives fresh water. In 1989, Steven Spielberg shot *Indiana Jones and the Last Crusade*, starring Harrison Ford and Sean Connery, at the three-kilometer corridor, known as the Siq, which lies within Petra. Over millennia, many people including Moses and Cleopatra have come to Petra. Consider the Scotsman David Roberts who sketched numerous pictures of Petra in the 1840s. Or T. E. Lawrence, who visited when he was an archaeologist excavating *Krak des Chevaliers* castle. After living in *Bilaad ash Sham*, he helped organize the Arab Revolt in 1917. What follows is generally what happened.

CUT TO:

CAMERA is running forward, toward a camp where four people are seated around a large bonfire. Sound mix: Hear men's laughter, shouts of Happy New Year! Women singing, "The Eyes of Texas Are Upon You."

CUT TO:

CLOSE-UP of a cooler filled with American beer and an empty Stolichnaya quart bottle. PAN the party scene. Dozens of men have passed out from drink. Two men are still awake and shouting.

CUT TO:

AHMED

(RIPS OFF KEFFIYEH, FLINGS IT INTO THE FIRE)
I am Ahmed Galayet

and I want to drink whiskey!

I am Ahmed Galayet

and I want to drink whiskey!

I am Ahmed Galayet

and I want to drink whiskey!

CUT TO:

LEANNE

(LOOKS DIRECTLY INTO THE CAMERA)

I should probably explain that *Galayet Bandora* is a kind of tomato stew with garlic, onions, pine nuts, and spices. I think Ahmed is trying to say his last name, Ghazali. When the liquor ran out, Mindy and I stopped singing country western songs. The partiers grew morose. And then there was the fire. An accident really. Ahmed's keffiyeh really stoked the flames, and all the BBQ and extra potato salad burned to a crisp. We decided to drive back to Wadi Musa. Sadly, Ahmed wouldn't ride with us, instead he wrecked his brother's truck, a Mercedes-Benz, when he swerved to miss a stray donkey. I'm happy to report that the donkey lived, but the truck died a horrible death. As for me, I vowed to never bring spirits to another BBQ in the Arabian Desert. Ever.

FADE OUT

Yaa Jordan, Yaa 'Ayouni

And then suddenly the story is over there in the West Bank, February 25, 1994. An Israeli settler named Burach Goldstein, an American formerly of Brooklyn, New York, opened fire on unarmed Palestinians as they prayed inside the Ibrahim Mosque at the Cave of the Patriarchs in Hebron. The West Bank town is still in mourning. Anguish is everywhere. Goldstein killed

29 worshippers and wounded another 125 using an IMI Galil assault rifle. He carried four magazines of ammunition that held 140 rounds. Imagine: he shot many of them in the back. When Goldstein ran out of bullets, survivors attacked him and he was beaten to death. Now he's a martyr to the extremists in Israel. For Arabs, Goldstein is seen as the embodiment of a two-headed snake, American and Israeli.

For the present Jim cannot leave our flat. Although he's lived a decade of his life in the Middle East, and he's more acculturated than most Americans living here, it's too dangerous for him to go outside. He will be read in public as *Ajnabee*. Stranger, white male. American. Yesterday, a blond-haired German was stabbed in the neck as he walked through the *Balad*, downtown Amman. It was a case of mistaken identity; the Jordanian attacker thought the German was American like Burach Goldstein, the assassin in Hebron. Again, what we manifest on the outside is the constructed identity we must live with. Until tensions ease, I will do the marketing and go out in public. I resemble the people of Jordan and can pass unnoticed if I don't speak. Our landlord, a Palestinian from Tulkaram, a northern city in the West Bank, stopped by the flat and said that he and his family would watch over us. "You are under my roof and your safety is my family's concern," said Mr. Zu'hair. "I've called my brothers, and our families know you are not responsible for what happened in Hebron."

I understand that we are living among people who feel it is their duty to take care of us as guests. Mr. Zu'hair and his family have taken full responsibility for us even though we're foreigners, Americans. People from a nation-state that gave the world Tomahawk missiles and Apache helicopters. (Ironies abound.)

Later that day, I walked to the Souk for supplies. All I could think of was that the most painful experiences—loss of identity, abandonment, betrayal—are the momentums of change. But what if these are the teachers of rebirth?

FINAL SCENE, FADE IN:
Hubble Space Telescope image of the blue green orb, Earth, from outer space. Photomontage of hundreds of images of Oklahoma, New Orleans, Wyoming, San Francisco, Jerusalem, Japan, Romania, Jordan, to punctuate the meaning of the book. The images should be a mash-up of times and space/lands, day or night, and illustrate the author's life.

LEANNE (V.O.)

Hallucinating again. So hot I crawl back into that hospital room in Bethany, Oklahoma. An ancient old lady dressed in a white nightgown, her fuzzy white hair a mop, and she's in the hospital bed next to mine, and there's no room in the children's ward so I'm here, and she's panting hard as if she's been running across the dirt playground toward the WA-HE Cafe, and they come in and drain a dishpan of her lung's bubbly juices, but I can't focus; the searing heat makes me float up and I hear them all say that she is dying, and I am dying and what a shame it is; and she does die and I die too. Twinned, we float away on petals of glorious pale yellow to places I've never seen before. My body a changed being, I wave hello and good-bye to both my mothers and all my future descendants swimming in the waters of the blue green orb, and at last we coalesce; at last, peace.

FADE OUT

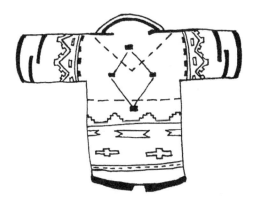

Embodied Tribalography – First Installment

The stories in *Choctalking on Other Realities* are an embodied tribalography, meaning I've carried them for decades, maybe for generations. They show not only how one thing leads to another, but that movement across space and time, i.e., travel, transforms us into something more than we were. Here, I return with a renewed sense of wonder to Degenawidah and Ayonwatha, the remarkable two-man team that united warring tribes into the Haudenosaunee Confederacy. In writing "The Story of America, A Tribalography," I was originally struck by the fact that Degenawidah and Ayonwatha's travels across the Northeast changed the world for the Haudenosaunee and their story of unification influenced the Founding Fathers in how they unified the thirteen colonies. But what is missing from the "Story of America" is a discussion of reciprocal embodiment between people and land as part and parcel of a tribalography. For example, if Degenawidah and Ayonwatha were the embodiment of the land's desire for peace, expressed through their actions (and I think they were), how might embodiment be expressed in other lands by other peoples?

When I was writing *Miko Kings, an Indian Baseball Story* (2007) it seemed to me that the southeastern Natives in the novel not only embodied the world and land of the story but that their physical movements emplotted the land with triumph, tragedy, renewal, and return. All attributes of survival. The story of *Miko Kings* also led me to research how an ancient Native Ballgame could be linked to earthworks sites in the Western Hemisphere and the cosmic world.[1]

In ferreting out these connections, I considered many factors and sources: the earthworks where the ancient games took place, the stylized iconography of the Southeastern Ceremonial Complex found at Mississippian sites, historical documents, oral traditions, and the way contemporary Native communities continue to play in tribal tournaments (that assist in our survival). I also reflected on the motion of water and wind in the Northern Hemisphere. This may explain why Natives in the Southeast dance counter-clockwise and would create an Indigenous ballgame played counter-clockwise, mimicking or expressing water flow, tornado, and hurricane winds. Further, the game is without time limits, evoking the four cardinal directions and, most importantly, it is an egalitarian game that anyone could play with a ball and a stick. I want to state right up front that while the manifestation of baseball expresses southeastern Indigenous lifeways—running the four directions counter-clockwise, imposing no time limits, having a pitcher in the center of play, much like the Choctaw ceremonial center pole, *iti fabassa,* which unites all three worlds—I'm not suggesting the Americans "stole" baseball from Indians. Rather, I'm saying that if the land taught Natives how to play ball, it just might have taught Non-Natives as well.

Fox, Deer, Rabbit, Turtle, Bear, Eagle, and Bat: "All My Relations Play Ball"

While some baseball historians track the origins of baseball to everywhere but Native America, Indigenous peoples can point to ancient ball fields situated next to earthworks sites throughout the Western Hemisphere. The fields of geometric shapes in the Americas suggest Indigenous peoples were playing ballgames adjacent to mound sites at a time that was simultaneous to their construction.

There are also ancient stories of how the animals and birds taught Natives how to play ball. The following is a compilation of stories I've heard and taken from the written sources I've read, and it is greatly abbreviated.[2]

A long time ago, the animals challenged the birds to a great ballgame, and the birds accepted. The captain of the animal team was Bear, and he was very strong. He could play all day and never get tired. All the way to the ball ground Bear was throwing logs and boasting how the animals would win the game.

The birds had Eagle for a captain, and the co-captain was Hawk. They were so fast they could carry the ball and fly it home to score a point. Everyone knew the birds were fast and powerful ball players. Before the big game the animals and the birds had an all-night dance. At that dance a few of the little ones came along and said they wanted to participate on the teams. Because they were so small, no one wanted them on the teams. Finally, Eagle took pity on the little ones and decided to make wings for the little ones so they could play the game too. Eagle took a small piece of leather from a drum and put it on Bat to make him wings. Next he stretched the fur of Squirrel to make him wings. Each of the little ones had a different way of fitting into the ballgame.

On the day of the big game, the little ones would prove the effort to give them wings was worth it. The two teams, animals and birds, played all day and all night. The game continued. Finally after many days and nights—when Bear and Eagle were exhausted—it was Bat who carried the ball and threw it in to score the winning point. For his hard work and humbleness,

> Bat was thought to be so important to both animals
> and birds that today he can play on both teams.[3]

This story of the animals and the birds has always been thought
to be about southeastern stickball, *toli*. But I suggest there may
be deeper meanings intended for listeners. The animals and
birds agree to play a ballgame, but they do not carry sticks to
use in the game (nor is a bat mentioned). Just before the big
game they host a party and an all-night dance. Outsiders show
up, but they're small and puny. Eagle, the most gifted leader
of the birds, offers them a spot on the bird's team, but they
must first be outfitted appropriately. For Bat, special wings are
made from a drum's leather. Squirrel's fur is reshaped to make
wings. After the changeup ceremony, Bat and Flying Squirrel's
new regalia make them proper for play on the birds' team. A
long and tiring game follows. When the animals and birds are
exhausted, it's the adopted-in-kin, either Bat or Flying Squirrel
(depending on the storyteller), who flies the ball across the goal
to win the game.

Here I'm interested in the story elements that deal with the
body and with physical movement. The story tells of transformation from one form into another and from movement in two
worlds, upper (flight) and middle (on the ground), and about an
adoption of form very different from one's own. The transfor-
mations of both Bat and Squirrel are a result of their desire to
play in a ballgame. The evolution of their bodies occurs quickly;
they suddenly embody new physical attributes, but they must
also remember how to move in their non-transformed selves,
occupying both worlds, in order to play in the game. Even
more profound, Indigenous southeastern storytellers have
always mapped Squirrel and Bat together in Ballgame's story,
often substituting one animal for the other. So it should come
as no surprise that scientists now suggest that 55 million years
ago, the bat and the squirrel shared an arboreal, squirrel-like
gliding ancestor,[4] underscoring a core southeastern belief that
"everything is related to everything."[5]

Other aspects of the story point to lessons Natives must embody, such as generosity and hospitality. Eagle offers "the little ones" a place on his team. The subtext: never underestimate those you think are less fortunate, for they may play harder for your team (read tribe) than your own kind. The story teaches us that dance is ceremonial and an integral part of momentous events, a cultural lifeway southeastern Natives have continued into the twenty-first century.

The story encourages Natives to perfect our bodies in order to attain a larger goal as Squirrel and Bat did. While the animals and birds' story teaches Natives to play a ballgame, we must remember that the game is unspecified and could mean any number of Indigenous ball games that require a team ethic. Finally, Natives learn through story that we're capable of embodying the knowledge of animals and birds.

What else can we infer from the story? It's not a story of warfare. No one is killed during play. No horrendous fights take place after the game, at least none we're told about. The birds and animals also show us how to make fictive kin with people and things (read systems) different from ourselves. This is also something that the Iroquois Condolence Ceremony teaches.

In the historic Southeast there are many examples of Choctaw fictive kin traveling on diplomatic missions on behalf of our tribe. Fictive kin is a term used by scholars to describe kinship that is from neither blood ties nor marriage. The Choctaws have a very old and prominent Fani Mingo/Miko (squirrel chief) institution that serves as a kind of cultural template for diplomacy. Fani Mingo/Miko, often an adopted outsider, must "play" as hard for the opposing team as he does for his "home" team, just as Bat and Squirrel played for their adopted team. In other words, Fani Mingo/Miko must advocate for the tribe or town he is not a member of. As Patricia Galloway points out:

> These first explorers found native institutions in place for dealing with formal intertribal communication. In the early eighteenth century the *fani mingo* institution served this purpose among the Chickasaw

and Choctaws; tribes would adopt an advocate within a neighboring tribe, and his duty would be to argue in favor of what became in a sense his adopted tribe whenever war threatened to break out. Under other names such an institution may have been widespread as a means of dealing with intertribal relations throughout the Southeast, connected with the fictive kinship mechanisms of the calumet ceremony.[6]

The story of the animals and birds shows us how to make diplomatic relations with other tribes and foreigners, those different from ourselves, that will aid in our survival.

Mounds as Storied Bodies

Since April 2011, I've been one of the team of playwrights and theatre scholars working on a research project, "Indigenous Knowledge, Contemporary Performance," which involves developing new Indigenous performance models based dramaturgically on Indigenous cultural texts. The Social Sciences and Humanities Research Council of Canada (SSHRC) awarded the project grant to five playwrights (including myself) and three theatre scholars. The grant is housed at Guelph University in Canada. The Indigenous performance model that Monique Mojica (Kuna and Rappahannock) and I hope to create employs the deep structure of earthworks as dramaturgical models. What we mean is that mounds were built by layering different kinds of soils one upon the other. In our play, soil layering will be represented in the stories we layer. As I have written in other essays, we began our research at mound sites by asking the question: Do Natives embody the land of their origin? To help with our research we talked with tribal elders and residents in Native communities in close proximity to mounds sites.

We also visited mound sites from Canada to Louisiana, and many sites in between. They vary in ages from the Archaic, Early Woodland, Middle Woodland, and late Woodland/Mississippian periods. In the Southeast some of the great mound cities are Poverty Point (Louisiana), Moundville (Alabama),

Nanih Waiya (Mississippi), and Okmulgee (Georgia). Other earthworks known as Hopewell era sites are located across Ohio and the Ohio Valley. At one time, hundreds of thousands of mounds, including embankments, conical mounds, platform mounds, and effigy mounds, dotted Indigenous North America, beginning as early as 4000 BCE. The very name "Turtle Island" connotes a vast effigy mound rising out of the water.

In studying the mounds as Indigenous literatures, we asked a second question: are earthworks embodied mnemonics aligned with moon and sun rotations to show future generations of Natives when and where to converge at specific sites? Consider, for example, the Newark Earthworks site in Ohio, which is the largest surviving Hopewell complex: One of its mounds, the Octagon Earthworks, comprises a type of lunar observatory for tracking "the motions of the moon, including the northernmost point of the 18.6-year cycle of the lunar orbit. The moon then rises within one-half of a degree of the octagon's exact center."[7] Today an 18.6-year lunar cycle of return continues to be marked in ceremony by Natives and Non-Natives wishing to witness the moonrise. But most often they must stand outside the Octagon Earthworks, which lies within a privately held golf course. In ancient times what kinds of community activities would Indigenous people have developed to complement the lunar return? One answer: ball games.

Consider the Bird Mound at Poverty Point, Louisiana, one of the major earthworks sites that Monique Mojica and I visited. Located near West Carroll Parish, Louisiana and fifteen miles from the Mississippi River on the Macon Bayou, Poverty Point is one of the Western hemisphere's largest earthworks and is relatively close to the Choctaw's mother mound, Nanih Waiya, only 197 miles away.

Built during the late Archaic period, Poverty Point is home to the 3,600 year-old Bird Mound. While archaeologists say they do not know why Mound A, or Bird Mound, came into being, I suggest a possible explanation as to why the mound was built in such a short period of time, and what this may signify.

Natives at Poverty Point used all means available to them, from the sacred to the scientific. Astronomers, mathematicians, geologists, engineers (for soil analysis and design), storytellers, the young and the old all came together to create the mound in approximately three months.[8] Natives in the Southeast literally moved a mountain of soil, some 238,000 cubic meters *in approximately 90 days,* to create the story of the Bird Mound.

Let's pause for a moment: Natives built Bird Mound in three months. What would have been the significance of 90 days to these people that they would demand such labor of themselves? The Bird Mound faces west and her wings seem tilted downward, as if landing. Her head may have tilted to one side, but it's impossible to know as her head has been dug away by nineteenth century looters looking for gold. However the angle of the wings could signify that she's moving to perch in order to be mounted by a mate.

The giant Bird Mound earthworks has a wingspan of 640 feet and stands seven stories high. Considering the size of the effigy, it seems likely that she's a bird of prey, a red-tailed hawk. Red-tailed hawks embody special meanings for southeastern Natives, especially Choctaws. The red-tailed hawk is a solar bird, one of power and strength, and the tail feathers are bright red in sunlight. Red signifies lifeblood and is sometimes a powerful metaphor for war.

Red-tailed hawks mate over a period of a few days in late winter or early spring. By March, the female lays her eggs, one every other day, so two eggs will take up to four days. The incubation period for hawk eggs is typically 35 days. It generally takes another four days for the small nestlings to hatch out of their shells. Once out of their shells, the nestlings will spend another 46 days or so in the nest before the baby birds begin to leave on short flights. The total time needed to create a red-tailed hawk, from mating to a fledgling leaving the nest, is approximately 90 days. *Three months.* Therefore, it would seem that Bird Mound at Poverty Point is possibly a performance mound that embodies the story of the red-tailed hawk from birth to first flight—the story of its creation. I suspect that the people who came together, from many directions, to write the story of Bird Mound into the land must have considered her an important symbol for their communities.

And yet, there's more to the story. Bird Mound signals two major ceremonial events: March 21, the Vernal Equinox, and June 21, the Summer Solstice, and it may also be read as a mnemonic expression of a return to home base—the subtext of Native Ballgame. If a red-tailed hawk's eggs were laid in March, the fledglings would be ready to leave the nest sometime in late June, close to the time of the Summer Solstice. Traditionally, Choctaws (and other southeastern tribes) extinguished all "fires" on Summer Solstice, known as *Luak Mosholi*. Fires being a multi-purpose metaphor for settling all scores, ending the old six-month cycle and beginning a new cycle that will end on Winter Solstice.

The ceremonial cycles are not the only functions of the Bird Mound, but again, if we connect the gestation of an actual bird, a red-tailed hawk, with the building of a bird's mound, a performance of natural and cosmic events begins to unfold at the site. We can *see* the ceremonial event; the mound rises above the horizon and spreads its wings, a story to be read over and over again for all who visit.

Other important performance features at Poverty Point are the dance grounds, ball fields, a small flat-topped ball court, six elliptical half-rings that if laid end to end would span seven and one-half miles, and a series of circular holes for oak posts that archaeologists believe were a calendar. Again, the calendar marks ceremonial times for *ever-returning events* at that site, which may have instructed Native visitors when the annual gatherings and ballgame tournaments would occur.

Poverty Point also contains many icons: jasper owls, a large bird of prey, panther, Fox Man, and Long Tails, all which could represent ancient clans or even ball teams that came to the site seasonally. Much more research will be needed to form a better picture of the past, but at Native Fastpitch tournaments in Oklahoma today, panther and hawk, even tornado and hurricane (again symbolizing the wind currents in the Northern Hemisphere), are but a few of the Native team symbols worn by modern ball players. Just as copper and shell icons once worn or carried by southeastern Natives symbolized clan, tribe, (or team affiliation), I suggest the accouterments of Native Ballgame express the continuity of culture embodied in everyday contemporary Native life: a return home.

Ancient replications of ball fields figure in the shell gorgets as well. One style, the Cox Mound gorget, found in both Tennessee and Alabama, has four engraved woodpecker heads facing counter-clockwise around a square ground, with a crossed point within a circle. As has been previously discussed, Native Ballgame is played counter-clockwise on a geometric-shaped ball field, and our dances are also performed counter-clockwise. Therefore, the cross within a circle in these ancient icons may encompass both ballgame motifs *and* ceremonial dances, but more importantly the engraving may replicate the wind and water systems that move counter-clockwise in the Northern Hemisphere.

According to anthropologist F. Kent Reilly III in "People of Earth, People of Sky: Visualizing the Sacred in Native American Art of the Mississippian Period,"[9] the Native universe of the Mississippian period had stories about three important mythic zones.

One may conceive of the relationship among these overlapping mythic cycles much as an environmental scientist perceives overlapping environmental zones. The transitional area where zones overlap—what ecologists call an ecotone—possesses the most wide-ranging biodiversity. Analogously, the area where these mythic cycles overlap, in effect, constitutes a religiously charged ecotone in which various Mississippian cosmogonic beliefs thrive. Aspects of these three mythic zones unquestionably survive today in the traditional beliefs and religious rituals of certain contemporary Native American groups.[10]

Following Reilly's logic, I suggest that these ecotones can still be found on the ball diamonds located on tribal grounds such as the Choctaw's Red Warrior Park at Tuskahoma, Oklahoma. Native Ballgame has morphed over time into Fastpitch Softball. In fact, the ball games are the reason so many families return to Tuskahoma each Labor Day.

Reilly's interpretation relies on the research of the excavated artworks found at southeastern Mississippian-era mound sites. "The Native American universe of the Mississippian period, in which ideological as well as historical action occurred, was a three-leveled configuration composed of the Above World or Overworld (i.e., the sky), the Middle World, and the Beneath World or Underworld." Reilly goes on to say (I'm paraphrasing) that the central axis connected all these worlds.

The story of the center pole (that unites all three places at once) is also told to explain how the Choctaws and Chickasaws became two tribes. Each night the pole was placed in the ground to determine which way the tribe should travel; but eventually they argued about which way it was leaning and split into two groups. In Choctaw, the ceremonial center pole is sometimes commonly referred to as *iti fabassa*. The "Pole Man" is called *Tikba heka*, the one who gives the cry preceding Ballgame's dance.

Another important aspect of Poverty Point was trade. According to archaeologist Jon Gibson, "long-distance trade was a hallmark of Poverty Point culture. Stones were carried over long distances up to 1,400 miles. Many kinds of materials were traded, including flint, sandstone, slate, shale, granite, and other coarse igneous rocks, soapstone, crystal quartz, copper, and galena."[11] While corn is not in the archaeological record, other foods such as persimmons, wild grapes, wild beans, hackberries, doveweed, fish, and birds such as sandhill cranes, turkeys, geese, herons, and crows were found in the ashes at the dig sites. Also found there was the medicinal herb snakeroot, an important trade good in the Southeast, especially among Native ball players.

Mounds, Ball Games and Snakeroot

Seventy-three-year-old Choctaw ball player Sim Noah from Battiest, Oklahoma, tells it this way. He says he played all positions in baseball but mostly pitcher, catcher, first baseman, and outfielder. He played baseball in the fields that his father cleared in the mid-1930s around Battiest, and he says his father and his uncles also played ball, as did his grandfather *and* grandmother. Noah adds that he and his family played ball on the first cleared ball fields at Tuskahoma in the Choctaw Nation's Red Warrior Park over fifty years ago. Today the Choctaw Nation continues to host a yearly Labor Day Fastpitch Tournament at Tuskahoma and invites tribal teams from all over the country to come and play ball there.

Noah says that back in the early 1960s, he and his friends needed to raise money for the entrance fees to a nearby baseball tournament, so they gathered snakeroot. "Once," he says "we were on strike from our jobs and a bunch of us went out and dug snakeroot to get enough money to play in a ball tournament. We sold snakeroot to the general store. They said they'd pay us $25.00 per pound. Snakeroot is light, so it took some doing to get enough money, but we did it. We wanted to play ball. And we did," he says smiling. "I have the trophy that's three feet high in the garage, still."

Sim Noah's story shows how he and his friends strategized and collaborated to harvest a plant they could exchange for enough money to play in a ballgame tournament. They walked the fields around Battiest and collected the snakeroot. The local general store owner then sold the snakeroot to local Choctaws to use for medicinal purposes and for making turpentine. All this snakeroot economy in 1960 was going on in an area of mostly Choctaw towns. Yet the practice of gathering snakeroot by southeastern Natives dates back hundreds of years, as evidenced by the writings of an eighteenth century Frenchman.

In his memoir on the history of Louisiana, Antoine Simon Le Page du Pratz wrote on the uses of the "rattle-snake-herb."[12] Du Pratz says that the plant was used to cure victims of snakebites: "…it is the specific remedy against the bite of that dangerous reptile."[13] He reports that Natives would chew a piece of the root for a while, apply it to the wound, and wait for the ill effects to subside. During his sixteen years in the Lower Mississippi Valley (1718-1734) du Pratz lived near two waterways, Bayou St. John and St. Catherine's Creek, a small southwesterly stream that joined the Mississippi. As everyone in the South knows, where there's water, there are edibles for snakes, such as frogs, small mammals, and birds. It seems likely that du Pratz and his Indian friends were also gathering snakeroot to aid in the treatment of rattlesnake bites. We can extrapolate that snakeroot would likely have been a medicinal trade good for large gatherings and ceremonies that du Pratz witnessed. Therefore we know that gathering and trading snakeroot is a centuries old practice among southeastern Indians. In gathering snakeroot Noah and his teammates were continuing that tradition.

Another point to mention is that when ball players like Sim Noah and others retell a ballgame story, they often hold an imaginary ball while explaining specific physical movements of a ball player they remember. Sometimes they show in a kind of slow motion how a player used his or her body in making certain plays work to their advantage. Anthropologist Brenda Farnell suggests that practiced movements evoke body memory and teach more than just perfected actions. "When body movements are viewed as action signs…they become one kind of semiotic practice among others, all of which provide persons with a variety of cultural resources for the creation of meaning. Dances and rituals are replete with these kinds of metaphorical gestures and, as we shall see, frequently extend to include whole body action signs and metaphorical usages of the ritual or other performance spaces."[14] Farnell suggests that the visual movements serve the tellers' memory of the story that's being passed along. The telling and showing of the moves by an elder ball player may seem rather informal or even happenstance to outsiders, but it nevertheless energizes younger players to join in the game. This may explain why Native Ballgame tournaments remain a powerful force among community members. In these multigenerational gatherings, younger generations are encouraged to be the future of the tribe's cultural practices, whether dancing, singing, or pitching a ball for the team.

Ballgame and Native Towns

How a ball game augments the development of Native towns and kinship networks among southeastern Indians is another part of the Ballgame story. Consider again Sim Noah and his ball playing teammates. They're from around Battiest, a small, unincorporated town in McCurtain County in southeastern Oklahoma. From Battiest, ball teams can travel five miles west to Pickens and pick up more players, or go six miles southeast to Bethel and play ball against the Bethel Braves' team. A little farther south and west is Hochatown, another Choctaw community that produces ball players. If we drive southeastward over to Wright City, a town whose economy has been devastated by the 2009 closing of Weyerhaeuser, an international forest products' company, you still can't swing a bat without hitting a Choctaw ball player. All of these towns in McCurtain County have large numbers of Choctaw ball-team families that still play in the annual Choctaw Nation's Fastpitch Tournament. In 2008, Lara Mann (Choctaw and poet) and I interviewed twenty-seven ballplayers and their families from around this region.[15]

Choctaw teams generally enter one or more tribal tournaments held at the Cherokee Nation, Muskogee Creek Nation, Seminole Nation, and Chickasaw Nation. Teams are multi-generational and often inter-tribal, with moms, dads, children, aunts, uncles, cousins and even grandparents traveling together in RVs, pick-ups, and buses to the various locations to play in tournaments and support their family teams. Yet, Native Ballgames in Oklahoma are largely unnoticed by mainstream newspapers, local television stations, and by Oklahomans in general. While working on Native Ballgame research, I asked dozens of Non-Native Oklahomans if they'd ever been to an All-Indian Fastpitch tournament to watch the ballgames, stickball, chunkey, or even Cherokee marbles. The answer is always the same: "I've never heard of them."

Kinship Vines and Native Ballgame Culture

Kinship among the Choctaw and Chickasaw peoples is deeply intertwined, connecting towns and communities throughout southeastern Oklahoma. In my novel *Shell Shaker* (2001), I wove Choctaw and Chickasaw families together in order to better explain our past. In *Miko Kings* I wove together Choctaw and Chickasaw ball players to explain an aspect of the present.

Here's what I mean: Ashley Hart (Choctaw Chickasaw) from Ada, Oklahoma, was a shortstop for Native All-Stars, a Choctaw-Chickasaw Ada team. The Native All-Stars played in the women's division at the Choctaw Nation's Fastpitch Tournament in 2005 and were interviewed for a short documentary film James Fortier and I were co-producing, titled *Playing Pastime: American Indians, Fastpitch Softball and Survival*[16]. Ashley's father and mother both coach Native Fastpitch teams. At the time of the interview, Ashley was the president of the Native American Student Association at East Central University in Ada, Oklahoma. Her sister married Jason Wallace (Chickasaw), a player for the ball team Red Storm. A year or so after we finished *Playing Pastime*, Ashley married ball player Jeremy Wallace (Chickasaw), brother of Jason, also from Ada. So two Choctaw-Chickasaw sisters married two Chickasaw brothers, and both families are well-known ball players supporting a number of teams at the Choctaw Nation's Fastpitch Tournament, the Chickasaw Nation's Fastpitch Tournament, and other local tournaments.

In the film we interviewed Pauline Walker, Jeremy and Jason's 93-year-old grandmother. She told us that she began playing stickball as a girl, and later baseball. Mrs. Walker's first language is Chickasaw, and at the time we filmed her, she was frequently traveling to Washington, DC, as a Chickasaw ambassador, accompanying Chickasaw Governor Bill Anoatubby. So, these families are participants in all cultural lifeways, even beyond Fastpitch. Jeremy Wallace worked for the Chickasaw Nation's Head Start program in Ada and was active in tribal cultural activities. He was one of the performers in the Chickasaw Nation's theatrical play *Hina Falaa*, the story of how the Choctaws and the Chickasaws (in ancient times) became two tribes. The play was written and performed by Chickasaw actors, dancers and singers; Chickasaw composer Jerod Tate wrote the original musical score. The Chickasaw Nation produced the play in 2009 for a standing-room-only crowd at the 1089-seat Hallie Brown Ford Fine Arts Center at East Central University in Ada. Dozens of Chickasaws and Choctaws performed in the cast and crew; the Chickasaw Nation also produced a DVD and a CD of *Hina Falaa*.

The play's subtext is that the population was large enough to split, and like a single cell dividing to reproduce, one group became two tribes. The story tells us that the split happened peacefully. Just as in the story of the animals and birds there is no warfare. It would seem good ethics can be learned from a ballgame story.

Native ball playing families like the Harts and the Wallaces remain active in cultural ceremonies through intertwined tribal networks. Today, the Wallace family is large enough to divide into several Fastpitch teams: Twister, Red Storm, and Mulihoma.[17] And yes, Choctaw dancers, dancing counter-clockwise, are part of the opening day ceremonies at Tuskahoma.

To say that Native Ballgame tournaments play a role in growing Native populations in the twenty-first century is stating the obvious. As evidenced in their report to the Oklahoma Indian Affairs Commission in 2011, the Chickasaw Nation now boasts a population of 49,000 Chickasaws. They also report that their operations include seventeen casinos, eighteen smoke shops, a chocolate factory, several museums, a publishing house, and a host of other businesses with a combined annual tribal economic impact of thirteen billion dollars.[18]

The Choctaw Nation's website reports that the tribe employs 7,600 tribal and non-tribal Oklahomans. The tribe's overall population has grown to 223,279 Choctaws worldwide; 84,670 in-state.[19] Compare this to the paltry population of 18,981, the number of Choctaws reported in the final Dawes Rolls of 1894.[20] Obviously the Trail of Tears removal era, disease, boarding schools, and often malnutrition had taken its toll on the Choctaw population.

The tribal ballgame tournaments held by the Choctaw Nation, Muskogee Creek Nation, Seminole Nation, and Chickasaw Nation[21] are played on tribal lands during the tribes' national holidays, with hundreds of Native fans and families coming to watch the games. I've witnessed the Chiefs at the Muscogee Creek Nation and Chickasaw Nation (in the case of the Chickasaw Nation, the leader is titled 'Governor') give their State of the Nation's address *while* the ball games are being played on the field. This may seem disrespectful to the office of the leader, but let's consider what the ballgame expresses. Ball playing Indians running the bases counter-clockwise, adjacent to the site where a leader speaks as the metaphorical "center pole" of the tribe, may signal our ever-returning presence on the land, just as cosmic solar and lunar events are ever-returning at earthworks sites such as Newark, Poverty Point, and hundreds of mound complexes in the North Hemisphere. Indigenous games and literatures written on the land are the embodied stories that reinforce our presence as ever-alive and ever-returning.

Mainstream Oklahomans saying that they know nothing about Native ballgames being played at tribal tournaments doesn't mean the ballgames aren't being played. Same-same in the past three centuries. Du Pratz does make a brief note about Native games in his historical account. He says that one game was played with a pole eight feet long, another with three sticks eight or nine inches long, and that another ball game was played by the youth: "The young people, especially the girls, have hardly any kind of diversion but that of the ball: this consists in tossing a ball from one to the other with the palm of the hand, which they perform with a tolerable address."[22]

What I'm suggesting is that the Native Ballgame tournaments are a centuries old story of continuity, emplotted in the land, embodied by the players. And as du Pratz's observations indicate, even if Europeans did witness ball activity, they didn't understand its importance to Native life and culture.

While we don't yet have documented evidence of Native Ballgames being played next to mounds or around Choctaw towns in the eighteenth century, I hope for lost letters from the early colonial period. Perhaps they're in the archives, or in private collections waiting to be discovered. Historical recovery has no time limits.

Lands that Embodied Story and Play Off Systems

Certainly Choctaw place names were the memory aids of their day. The names suggest that important events happened there. Nearly every Choctaw town name reveals another story: *Kahtasha*, Fleas are There; *Halunlawansha*, Bullfrog Place; *Puskus Takali*; Hanging Child; or *Haanke Ullah*, Bawling Goose. According to Patricia Galloway, southeastern Natives coded place names with embodied meanings of events and non-events that had happened at those sites. "As we shall see the land was everywhere an integral part of the stories of Native nations, woven into history, cosmology, and moral discourse – hence 'emplotted': constructed cognitively as an active participant in the drama of human life."

In Patricia Galloway's book chapter, "A Storied Land,"[23] she explains why the early sixteenth-century Spanish and French tell an incomplete story of the documented place names they recorded because Native guides mostly led foreigners to connecting towns on well-worn foot and horse paths, missing much of the interior landscapes where mounds, ball fields, and dance grounds were located. If the foreigners never thought to ask about vast open spaces then there are no documented stories (read histories) about them. "To avoid this conundrum," writes Galloway, "we really need words, so we are forced to skip forward to the seventeenth and particularly the eighteenth centuries, to begin to hear Indian people characterize the land through the reportage of Europeans attempting to learn about it. And what we can now hear depends upon what the Europeans of that era wanted to know."[24]

Though very little is known at this time about Indigenous ballgame organizing systems, or the epistemological benefits to a people who played games in teams, anthropologist Greg Urban argues that moieties may have been a model for ballgame team organization since moieties also assigned burial roles and regulated marriages.[25] Perhaps. But I respectfully suggest that it's just as likely the other way around. Ball playing teams could have, over time (*longue durée*), helped develop the moieties. In team games, one side plays the other side. Eventually one person from one side (read: team) marries someone from the other side; same with burial practices. Play-off systems could have leeched into all aspects of cultural life.

For the past three decades historians and scholars have pointed out that Choctaws always exhibited a kind of "play-off system" when dealing with foreign powers. Historian Richard White makes the argument that Choctaws played the French against the English for much of the eighteenth century in order to benefit from trading for goods and guns.[26] According to Patricia Galloway and Clara Sue Kidwell, the Choctaws were trying to re-establish their play-off system between the

Spanish and English as late as 1771.[27] All this playing "one side against the other" for the advantages of the home team suggests the possibility that play-off systems had deep cultural roots embodied in Choctaws through the continued performance of ballgames. Again it may be time to consider the role of game-play as a progenitor of Choctaw political culture. As Brenda Farnell writes, "Once persons are conceived as embodied agents empowered to perform signifying acts with both speech and action signs, the way is clear to see the medium of movement as an equally available resource for meaning-making that can also be imaginative and metaphorical."[28] A play-off performed on a geometric ball field between teams could easily have been a primer for learned skills in dealings between Choctaw leaders and their French, English, or Spanish opponents. Political strategies learned through the praxis of ballgames aided in our survival over millennia.

One only has to look at the famous nineteenth-century Choctaw stickball ballplayer called *Tullock-chish-ko*, "He Who Drinks the Juice of the Stone," to see that even the mantle of his game-name reflects a survival story. [29]

Stories Ever-Living

Okay, back to embodied tribalography and the new and selected stories in this collection. Here in all the telling and retelling, I've moved across space and time, reflecting on how tribal people embody land and stories. In the process I found my distant ancestors, my mothers, my uncles, myself. At times my family's pain and my own sense of loss have knocked me to my knees; yet for a writer that's what it means to embody the stories we tell, perform, write, live.

In *Miko Kings* no matter what happened, the characters in the story returned home, just like ancient ball players returning to play on ball fields at earthworks sites. Ezol Day is the metaphorical *iti fabassa*, the center pole of the story of *Miko Kings*, ever-in-motion, connecting multiple worlds at once. In a way,

I guess Ezol Day embodies me, not the other way around. I have her to thank for teaching me how to express the embodied stories presented here in *Choctalking on Other Realities*. For me they're ever-alive, and I've tried to make them live for you.

Notes

1 I use "Native Ballgame," to mean an ancient southeastern Indigenous game played on the grounds around mound complexes. I suggest this game served as a unifier connecting the upper, middle, and lower worlds of the southeastern cosmology.

2 For three months in the fall of 2004, I lived on the Eastern Band of Cherokee Indian's Qualla Boundary and was privileged to hear Cherokee storyteller Jerry Wolfe tell the ball game story several times. For a written account of the ball game story see *Myths of the Cherokee and Sacred Formulas of the Cherokees*. James Mooney. Cherokee Heritage Books, Cherokee. 1982. Pgs. 286-287. Further readings include *Native American Legends: Southeastern Legends: Tales from the Natchez, Caddo, Biloxi, Chickasaw, & Other Nations*. George E. Lankford. August House, Little Rock. 1987; and *Myths and Tales of the Southeastern Indians*. John R. Swanton. University of Oklahoma Press, Norman. 1995.

3 A similar version of the story appears in "The Bases Are Loaded: American Indian and American Studies" co-authored by Carter Meland, Joseph Bauerkemper, LeAnne Howe, Heidi Stark. *American Studies Journal. Special Issue: Indigenous Peoples of the United States*. Vol. 46:3/4 (Fall-Winter 2005), #1. Editors, Norman Yetman, David M. Katzman, Bernard Alan Hirsh.

4 Nancy Simmons, "Taking Wing", *Scientific American*. 299 (2008): 96-103

5 A quote by the late Choctaw writer and artist Roxy Gordon in "The Story of America: A Tribalography" in *Clearing a Path: Theorizing the Past in Native American Studies*, Routledge Press, New York. Nancy Shoemaker, Ed. 2001. Pgs. 29-48.

6 Patricia Galloway, *Choctaw Genesis, 1500-1700* (Lincoln: University of Nebraska Press, 1995), p. 322.

7 wikipedia.org/wiki/Newark_Earthworks

8 Kidder, Tristram R.; Ortmann, Anthony L; Arco, Lee J. (November 2008) "Poverty Point and the Archaeology of Singularity." *Society for American Archaeology: Archaeological Record* 8: (5): 9-12.

9 *Hero, Hawk, and Open Hand*, Richard Townsend, Robert Sharp, eds. Yale University Press, New Haven and London. 2004. pp/ 125-139.

10 Ibid. Pg. 126-127.

11 *Poverty Point*. Jon Gibson. Louisiana Archaeological Survey and Antiquities Commission. 1999. No 7. Pg 22.

12 *The History of Louisiana*. Translated from the French of M. Le Page du Pratz. Louisiana State University Press. Baton Rouge. 1975. Pg. 251.

13 Ibid.

14 Brenda Farnell. "Metaphors We Move By." *Visual Anthropology 8* (2–4): 311–35. 1996. Pg. 323.

15 In 2008, we conducted research for a creative non-fiction book on Native Ballgame and its history. We interviewed contemporary ball players and learned about tournament play, and include a collection of historical newspaper accounts about nineteenth-century Indians and baseball, and Fastpitch softball culture.

16 For more on American Indian Fastpitch softball, players and their families, see the twenty-eight-minute documentary *Playing Pastime, American Indian Softball and Survival,* 2006, co-produced by James Fortier, and LeAnne Howe. Contact Turtle Island Productions, http://www.turtle-island.com/ for information on how to order a copy.

17 Ashley Hart and Jeremy Wallace can both be seen playing ball in *Playing Pastime, American Indian Softball and Survival.*

18 http://www.ok.gov/oiac/documents/2011.FINAL.WEB.pdf

19 Ibid. The employment figures are taken from the Choctaw Nation's website: http://www.choctawnation.com/

20 Clara Sue Kidwell. *The Choctaws in Oklahoma: From Tribe to Nation, 1855-1970.* University of Oklahoma Press, Norman. 2008.

21 In the summer of 2005, I attended three Fastpitch softball tournaments: the Muskogee Creek Nation, the Choctaw Nation, and the Chickasaw Nation. The games were held during the national holidays of the tribes, and the chief's speeches were given as the ball games continued. In the case of the Chickasaw Nation, the games were rained out that were to continue during Governor Anotubby's speech. Lightening forced the Governor to postpone his speech.

22 *The History of Louisiana.* Translated from the French of M. Le Page du Pratz. Louisiana State University Press. Baton Rouge. 1975. Pg. 366.

23 Patricia K. Galloway. *Practicing Ethnohistory: Mining Archives, Hearing Testimonies, Constructing Narrative.* University of Nebraska Press. 2006. Pgs 175-201.

24 Ibid. Pg 176

25 Greg Urban. "The Social Organizations of the Southeast." In Raymond DeMallie and Alfonzo Ortiz, eds, *North American Indian Anthropology: Essays on Society and Culture.* Pgs. 172-93. University of Oklahoma Press, Norman. 1994.

26 Richard White. *The Roots of Dependency: Subsistence, Environment and Social Change Among the Choctaws, Pawnees, and Navajos.* University of Nebraska Press. Lincoln. 1983.

27 Patricia Galloway and Clara Sue Kidwell. "Choctaws in the East." In *Handbook of North American Indians: Volume 14. Southeast,* eds. Raymond Fogelson, William Sturtevant. Smithsonian Institution. Pgs 499-514. Washington D.C. 2004.

28 Brenda Farnell. "Metaphors We Move By." *Visual Anthropology 8* (2–4): 311–35. 1996.

29 *George Catlin: North American Indians.* Ed. Peter Matthiessen. Penguin Books. New York. 1989. Pg. 400.

Author's Note

I owe an enormous debt of gratitude to my editor Joan
Pinkvoss for her belief in my work (and for not pulling her hair
out while working with me) these past twelve years. Yakoke
Joan. The same shout out for Shay Brawn, Managing Editor
at Aunt Lute Books, and all the wonderful women that have
helped bring my work to life. Over the last decade or so, no
friend, or reader has been more supportive than Dean Rader.
Long before *Shell Shaker* appeared in print, he generously
read the manuscript-in-process and offered criticism and
insights. Others who have read and commented on my work-
in-process or offered solace include: Jodi Byrd, Robert Warrior,
Carter Meland, Joseph Bauerkemper, Carol Miller, Rigoberto
Gonzales, Tayari Jones, Chadwick Allen, Philip Morgan, Daniel
Justice, Jennifer Kidney, Carol Cornsilk, Ken Hada, Harvey
Markowitz, Sandra Soli, and all the Salonaires at Salon Ada.
Thanks dear friends. I especially want to thank Jim Wilson
who has read these stories in draft a jillion times and offered
advice and criticism. And finally for my sons Joseph Craig and
Randall Craig who, along with me, survive these stories.

Previously Published

"My Mothers, My Uncles, Myself," *Here First: Autobiographical Essays by Native American Writers*, eds. Brian Swann and Arnold Krupat, Modern Library, a Random House imprint, 2000.

"The Story of America: A Tribalography," *Clearing a Path: Theorizing the Past in Native American Studies*, ed. Nancy Shoemaker, Routledge Press, 2001.

"The Chaos of Angels," *Callalo, Native American Literature*, Vol. 17, Native Heritage Issue 1, Johns Hopkins University Press, 1994.

"Moccasins Don't Have High Heels," *American Indian Literature, Revised Edition*, ed. Alan Velie, University of Oklahoma Press, 1991.

"How I Lost Ten Pounds," first published as "Due Diligence: Or How I Lost Ten Pounds" in *The Kenyon Review*, Vol. XXXII, Issue 1, Winter 2010.

"Choctalking on Other Realities," *Cimarron Review*, Issue 121, ed. Michael Wilson, Oklahoma State University, October 1997.

All the pieces listed above were originally published in somewhat different form and have been revised and edited for this book.

LeAnne Howe is an enrolled citizen of the Choctaw Nation and writes fiction, poetry, screenplays, creative non-fiction, plays, and scholarship that primarily deal with American Indian experiences. In 2012, she was honored with the Lifetime Achievement Award by the Native Writers' Circle of the Americas. Her short fiction has appeared in *The Kenyon Review, Fiction International, Callaloo, Story, Yalobusha Review, Cimarron Review, Platte Valley Review,* and elsewhere, and has been translated into French, Italian, German, Dutch and Danish. Her first novel, *Shell Shaker,* received an American Book Award in 2002 from the Before Columbus Foundation. *Equinoxes Rouge,* the French translation, was the 2004 finalist for Prix Medici Estranger, one of France's top literary awards. Howe's most recent novel, *Miko Kings: An Indian Baseball Story,* was the Hampton University's Read-In-Selection for 2009-2010. In 2011, Howe was awarded the Tulsa Library Trust Award for her work as an American Indian writer in Tulsa, Oklahoma.

As a 2010-2011 William J. Fulbright Scholar, LeAnne Howe lived in Amman, Jordan, to research her forthcoming novel, set in Bilaad ash Sham, and Allen, Oklahoma. In December 2012, Howe received a USA Ford Fellowship of $50,000 to continue her research and to write *Memoir of a Choctaw Indian in the Arab Revolt, 1917.* She is a Professor of American Indian Studies and English at the University of Illinois at Urbana-Champaign.

Aunt Lute Books is a multicultural women's press that has been committed to publishing high quality, culturally diverse literature since 1982. In 1990, the Aunt Lute Foundation was formed as a non-profit corporation to publish and distribute books that reflect the complex truths of women's lives and to present voices that are underrepresented in mainstream publishing. We seek work that explores the specificities of the very different histories from which we come, and the possibilities for personal and social change.

Please contact us if you would like a free catalog of our books or if you wish to be on our mailing list for news of future titles. You may buy books from our website, by phoning in a credit card order, or by mailing a check with the catalog order form.

Aunt Lute Books
P.O. Box 410687
San Francisco, CA 94141
415.826.1300

www.auntlute.com
books@auntlute.com

This book would not have been possible without the kind contributions of the Aunt Lute Founding Friends:

Anonymous Donor
Anonymous Donor
Rusty Barcelo
Marian Bremer
Marta Drury
Diane Goldstein

Diana Harris
Phoebe Robins Hunter
Diane Mosbacher, M.D., Ph.D.
Sara Paretsky
William Preston, Jr.
Elise Rymer Turner